外教社◎大学生英语分级阅读（一年级）·有声版
诺贝尔桂冠作家小传
英汉对照

U0745347

荒诞与现实之间:品特传

BETWEEN ABSURDITY AND REALITY:
A BIOGRAPHY OF HAROLD PINTER

Edwina Pendarvis　著

方柏林　陈大为　译

上海外语教育出版社
外教社 SHANGHAI FOREIGN LANGUAGE EDUCATION PRESS

图书在版编目(CIP)数据

荒诞与现实之间：品特传(英汉对照)/(美)彭达维斯著；方柏林，陈大为译.
—上海：上海外语教育出版社，2010
(外教社大学生英语分级阅读.一年级.诺贝尔桂冠作家小传)
ISBN 978-7-5446-1555-6

I.荒… II.①彭… ②方… ③陈… III.①英语—汉语—对照读物
②品特，H.(1930~2008)—传记 IV.H319.4:I

中国版本图书馆CIP数据核字(2009)第174403号

出版发行：**上海外语教育出版社**
    (上海外国语大学内) 邮编：200083
电 话：021-65425300（总机）
电子邮箱：bookinfo@sflep.com.cn
网 址：http://www.sflep.com.cn http://www.sflep.com
责任编辑：刘 芯

印 刷：上海叶大印务发展有限公司
经 销：新华书店上海发行所
开 本：700×1000 1/16 印张12.5 字数190千字
版 次：2010年3月第1版 2010年3月第1次印刷
印 数：5 000册

书 号：ISBN 978-7-5446-1555-6 / K·0048
定 价：28.00元

本版图书如有印装质量问题，可向本社调换

读伟人传记 提高人文素养

阅读，对于提高一个人的文化、语言水平至关重要。阅读伟人的传记更能丰富读者的历史文化知识，提高人文素养，帮助确立自己的人生目标，因为任何一部好的传记必定会提供主人公所处的时代背景，描述他(她)的生活理想、奋斗精神，及其在做人从业道路上所做的种种选择。

两年前，上海外语教育出版社采纳了方柏林先生的选题申请，同意出版英汉对照"诺贝尔桂冠作家小传"系列读物，我感到十分高兴。后来方先生和编辑许高女士分别来信要我为丛书作序，我便欣然允诺。

这套传记丛书使我想起了自己的部分阅读经验。在我读英语本科时，国家正处极端时期，学生能从图书馆借阅的文科书籍，量少面窄。直至1978年国家实施改革开放，我等才有机会在本科教育中断十年后，重返母校当了研究生。在学校图书馆新辟的国外赠书阅览室里，我先后读到了一大批外国文人的英文传记，其中很多是诺贝尔奖得主，如英国文豪萧伯纳、美国剧作家奥尼尔、在中国长大的美国作家赛珍珠，还有爱尔兰的贝克特等。当时的感觉就像是一位口渴已久的长途跋涉者无意中获得了醇美的甘露，我一本接一本地不停阅读，有时还去寻找同一作家的不同传记以期获取更多信息并加以比较。书中描写这些文化巨人所作的人生探索，与之俱来的痛苦和欢乐，还有在他们身上折射出来的高贵与猥琐、智慧与愚昧、坚毅与动摇，以及他们如何面对成功和荣誉，如何看待给予与幸福等等，仿佛我是在向这些文化伟人作零距离采访。这些书不但开阔了我的视野，丰富了我的历史文化知识，更是滋润了我的心田，消除了我心无所依而产生的焦虑和饥渴，帮我建起自己的人格心性和修养。毫不夸张地说，这些书在很大程度上决定了我后半辈子的人生道路、事业选择和做人的样式。

"诺贝尔桂冠作家小传"系列丛书的预想读者，是中国高等院校低年级学生。大学低年级学生能在自己人生性格和价值观形成的关键时期，阅读世界文化英才的中英对照传记，在认识一批对人类发展产生过深远影响的作家的生平业绩和内心世界的过程中，提高自己的人文素养和人格心性的境界，而与此同时增强自己英语阅读和翻译的能力，这该是件多么令人向往和愉快的事情！

这套丛书与以往翻译引进的国外图书不同，它是真正专为中国读者"量身定做"、精心设计的读物。方先生、美国作家 Edwina Pendarvis 女士以及许编辑经过多次反复商讨，选定了一组他们认为是"最有代表性和影响力"、在中国具有相当知名度的诺贝尔文学奖得主。然后以Pendarvis女士为主的美国作家，用形象生动的英语撰写这些文豪的传记。在英语用词和语言难度上，他们都反复讨论协商，从细微处入手，努力为读者创造一个愉快美好的阅读体验。方先生等又把这些传记翻译成鲜活地道的中文，供读者作中英文对照阅读，使这套丛书增添了新的用途和意义。

我对丛书的创意者和翻译者方柏林先生有较多的了解，他出生在安徽桐城，是南京大学英语系的一位优秀校友。他中英文功底扎实，勤于思考，又有较长的在国内外学习、工作和生活的经历。出于兴趣爱好，他一直在繁忙的工作之余从事着文学写作和翻译。他诙谐幽默而不乏睿智的文章，不但在网络博客上拥有众多读者，也常被刊登在国内外一些重要杂志和报刊上。早年在国内读研究生时，他曾一边撰写关于品特戏剧语言的英文论文，一边参与翻译英文原著《赛珍珠文化传记》。此后他去美国大学深造和工作期间，独自翻译了《河湾》、《一个唯美主义者的遗言》、《老谋深算》、《万灵节》、《布鲁克林有棵树》等一批名家的获奖小说，由人民文学、译林、漓江等重要出版社出版。

英文主笔Pendarvis女士是美国诗人，她的英语创作，文笔生动细腻，文字精准洗练，特别适合英语学习者阅读。同时，她还是美国著名的特殊禀赋教育（gifted education）专家，专门研究如何对天资聪颖的青少年实施有效教育。这一背景使她能从青少年成长的角度，来叙述诺奖作家成年阶段所受到的种种影响，如阅读的书籍、交往的朋友、对他们产生影响的家人等等。获得诺贝尔文学奖的机遇可遇不可求，但一个人的成长，是可以影响和可以造就的。

获得诺贝尔文学奖的作家都是了不起的成功者，但生活中了不起的成功者不一定都是获得大奖的精英，他（她）们可以是平凡的普通人，通过大量阅读和实践，在人格培育和人文素养上成为了不起的成功者。他们知道获取，更懂得奉献，能在生活和事业的实践体验中，找到真正的人生意义和幸福。

这，我想是这套传记丛书的英文作者、中文译者和出版者真正想奉献给广大读者的。

刘海平

南京大学外国语学院前院长

全国美国文学研究会会长

2009年6月于南石皮弄

Table of Contents
目 录

Chapter One

THE LONDON BLITZ

伦敦闪电战

A long, shrill whistle pierced the night sky over London. Another whistle followed, then hundreds, all over the city. It was winter, 1940. Londoners had heard this sound many times since autumn when the Nazis[1] had started bombing the city. Familiar as the whistling sounds were to the men, women, and children huddled in darkened buildings or in the underground railway stations during an attack, the sound had lost none of its terror. It was the sound of a falling bomb. Each piercing whistle ended in an explosion.

Ten-year-old Harold Pinter crouched between his mother and father in the family's bomb shelter[2]. They all waited, listening, unable to talk or think about anything but how long the attack would last and whether they and the people they loved would survive. After what seemed an unbearable length of time, the attack ended. The drone[3] of the German airplane motors faded into the distance. Sirens sounded the "all clear[4]" signal.

Following his father, Pinter crawled out of the shelter. His father had been first to get out of the shelter because he'd been last to get in it. Harold's mother followed Harold. How they hated being cooped up[5] in that metal, coffin-like box! They

1. Nazis: *n.* (常用复数) 德国纳粹党, 法西斯分子
2. bomb shelter: *n.* 防空洞
3. drone: *n.* 嗡嗡的声音
4. all clear: 空袭警报解除信号
5. coop up: 监禁, 将…禁锢在狭小空间里

一阵深长而尖厉的哨音划破伦敦的夜空。紧接着又是一声, 随后成百上千哨音响彻伦敦。这是1940年冬天。自从9月份纳粹开始轰炸这座城市起, 伦敦人已经多次听到这声音。空袭时男女老少挤在黑暗的建筑物或是地铁站里, 虽然他们已对这哨音十分熟悉, 但恐惧感却丝毫未能减少。那是炸弹落下的声音。每一阵尖厉的哨音都以爆炸声结束。

10岁的哈罗德·品特蜷缩在父母之间, 一家人此时躲在自家的防空洞里。他们等待着, 聆听着, 没法说话, 也没别的念头, 脑子里只想着空袭会持续多久, 自己和亲人能否在空袭中幸免于难。挨了好久, 空袭才结束。德国飞机引擎的嗡嗡声消逝在远方。城市上空响起了空袭警报解除的信号。

品特跟着父亲, 爬出了防空洞。他的父亲最后一个进防空洞, 所以是第一个出来的。哈罗德的母亲跟着哈罗德也爬了出来。围在那棺材样的金属盒子里, 他们也受够了! 这盒子究竟比房子本身安全多少, 他们

weren't sure it kept them much safer than the house itself did. Still, they didn't dare take any more chances than they had to. Their home was in Hackney, in London's East End[1]. The East End usually got the worst of the attacks because that's where the docks were. The Nazis wanted to keep ships from entering and leaving England.

The Pinter family was among thousands of London families who lived through the worst aerial[2] attacks ever made on any city up to that time. This series of attacks by the Nazis was called a "blitz[3]", shortened from the German word "blitzkrieg", which meant "lightning war". It was a new type of warfare. More planes and bombs were used in these attacks than had ever been used before. The Germans' goal was to attack with such blinding force that it was as deadly as a lightning strike. They hoped to overwhelm and destroy the enemy in a very short time. Adolf Hitler, Chancellor of Germany and leader of the Nazi party, had led his country into war. After invading Norway, Poland, and France, the Germans attacked England. The attack started on the Dover shore[4] of that island nation. It then moved to inland cities. London was battered with thousands of bombs.

1. East End: 东伦敦, 伦敦东区 (为港口区, 多工人住宅)
2. aerial: *adj.* 大气的, 空中的
3. blitz: *n.* 是德语单词 blitzkrieg (意为闪电战争) 的简称
4. Dover shore: 多佛海岸, 位于英、法之间多佛海峡英国一侧, 是连接北海和英吉利海峡的海上通道

也说不准。不过, 他们可不敢心存侥幸, 只得呆在防空洞里。他们家在伦敦东区的哈克尼。伦敦东区是码头所在地, 纳粹想阻止舰船出入英国, 因此那里通常全遭受最为严重的空袭。

成千上万像品特这样的家庭经历了这场空袭。这是有史以来对一个城市最为严重的空袭。由纳粹发动的这一系列空袭被称作"闪电战"(blitz), 这是德语单词"闪电战争"(blitzkrieg)的缩写。这是种新型战争。空袭中使用的飞机和炸弹数量之多, 前所未有。德国人希望通过狂轰滥炸式的空袭, 形成雷击般的致命打击。他们希望在短时间内压倒并摧毁敌人。德国总理、纳粹党主席阿道夫·希特勒将德国带入了这场战争。进入侵挪威、波兰和法国之后, 德军空袭了英国。空袭从这个岛国的多佛海岸开始, 继而转入内陆城市。伦敦受到成千上万枚炸弹的狂轰滥炸。

Except for the many fires started by the bombs, London was dark from afternoon until morning during the blitz. A "blackout[1]" was in place all through the city whenever an attack was expected. This helped keep the bombers from knowing the exact location of particular buildings. To children and adults alike the awful sounds of the approaching airplane motors, the whistles made by the bombs, and the massive explosions were a nightmare made real. Many small children were terrified. The planes and their bombs were so powerful that even their parents couldn't protect them.

Harold, who was past the age when he thought his parents had godlike powers, was scared. But he wasn't terrified. Besides, like most of the older boys, he felt he had to put up a brave front[2].

This afternoon was only one of many afternoons he'd had to sit in the shelter for an hour or more. He had gotten so used to it, that by now, he didn't just pretend to be brave. He actually got bored, having to stay in the shelter so long. Now, stretching his cramped limbs, he glanced at his father, Jack, a city man who'd never fired a gun. He looked at his mother, Frances, cheerful and loving. They were dear to him, but he knew

1. blackout: *n.* 灯火管制
2. front: *n.* (用单数表示) 态度；举止；外表
   如：He put on a bold *front*.
   他装出大胆的样子。

闪电战期间，伦敦从下午到早晨都处在黑暗中，只有炸弹引起的火灾才带来一丝光亮。空袭来临时，整座城市进入灯火管制状态，以防盖炸机辨认出建筑物的具体位置。无论对大人还是小孩来说，飞机临近时恐怖的引擎声、炸弹的呼啸声和巨大的爆炸声，都仿佛噩梦变成了现实，把许多小孩子吓坏了。飞机和炸弹威力实在太大，连父母都哄不住孩子。

哈罗德已经过了把父母当神看的年纪，他也感到害怕，但并没有被吓破胆。和大多数大男孩一样，他觉得自己必须表现得勇敢些。

那天下午，如同往常一样，他不得不在防空掩体里坐上一个多小时。他已经习以为常，甚至不用故作勇敢了。在防空掩体里呆这么久了，他实在觉得很闷。他伸了伸抽筋的手脚，瞥了一下父亲杰克，一个从未开过枪的城里人。他再看看母亲弗朗西斯。母亲看上去令人愉悦而又充满爱心。父母是哈罗德的亲人，但是他知道，即便是他们也不能保证自己的安全。他又看了看莫里森防空掩体。

they couldn't keep him safe. He looked at the Morrison shelter[1], too. Though it had a steel plate as a top, it seemed a flimsy[2] barrier between himself and a bomb. The shelter was only six and a half feet long, four feet wide, and two feet high. Its wire mesh sides let the three crowded occupants see outside it.

This kind of shelter was common in homes that had no cellar. When the planes bombed near their neighborhood, the Pinters[3], like many other families, got into this box. Harold's father had assembled the shelter from parts provided in the kit sent by the government. Unable to do much more than this to protect themselves, their lives depended mostly on the British pilots in their small, agile fighter planes, harrying the big, clumsy bombers. On the British pilots and on luck.

Harold went to their front door, opened it and listened. Silence — not a peaceful silence, but a stunned silence. It didn't last long. Soon the streets were full of people hurrying to check on their friends and relatives and to see what damage had been done to homes and buildings. All too often in the past few months, they'd rushed to put out fires and pull vic-

1. Morrison shelter: *n.* 莫里森防空掩体，官方称作桌式（莫里森）防空掩体。由约翰·贝克设计，以英国内务大臣赫伯特·莫里森命名，是二战期间英国政府向公民派发的组装式防空掩体
2. flimsy: *adj.* 脆弱的，易坏的
3. the Pinters: 品特一家，英语中在姓名后加 s 表示某某一家人，如 the Johns 表示"约翰一家人"

这掩体有钢板做的顶，勉勉强强挡在他和炸弹之间。防空掩体只有 6.5 英尺长、4 英尺宽、2 英尺高，侧面是铁丝网，挤在里面的一家三口能看见外面。

这种防空掩体在那些没有地窖的家庭中很常见。每当飞机的轰炸临近时，同其他许多家庭一样，品特一家就躲进这盒子。哈罗德的父亲用政府派发的组装工具，组装出防空掩体。他们仅能靠这个保护自己了。他们的性命多半要靠英国飞行员。这些飞行员驾驶着机身轻巧而敏捷的战斗机，与硕大而笨重的德军轰炸机周旋。就这样，哈罗德他们的性命，半靠英国飞行员，半靠运气。

哈罗德走到前门，打开门听着，门外一阵寂静。这不是那种让人安宁的寂静，而是那种惊吓过后的寂静。就连这样的寂静也未持续很久。顷刻之间，街上熙熙攘攘。人们急着去找各自的亲友，去看住房和建筑物的受损情况。过去几个月里，他们常常一跑出防空洞就去扑灭大火，

tims out of the rubble.

Harold put on his wool jacket, "I'm going out. Back soon," he called to his parents. He hurried down the steps, before either of them could object.

In front of a house near the corner of his street, he met one of his schoolmates. His schoolmate pointed. Smoke poured out of a house farther down the block, toward the docks. The two boys headed that way to see how bad things were and to help if they were needed. As usual, they looked for "ack ack" shells[1] as they walked. Ack ack shells — named for the sound the anti-aircraft guns made — were small treasures. All the boys wanted them either to save or to trade for some other little treasure. As the two friends got closer to where bombs had struck, they breathed in the smell of burnt wood. Soon, with every step, they felt the crunch of glass underfoot.

It was hard to believe this was the neighborhood where they'd played since they were old enough to play outside. Before the blitz, the Hackney neighborhood had been a busy, friendly place. The houses on this street were cozily close together and so close to the street that there were no side yards or front yards, only backyards

1. ack ack shells: *n.* 阿克阿克弹壳，因防空机枪 "阿克阿克" 的声音而得名，防空机枪因此也叫做 "阿克阿克枪"

或是从废墟里拯救幸存者。

哈罗德穿上羊毛夹克。"我出去一下。很快回来，"他对父母说。父母尚未来得及拒绝，他就已匆忙跑下台阶。

在街角一座房子前，他碰见了一位同学。在同学指点下，他看到街上靠近码头的一所房子上冒出了浓烟。两个男孩一起朝那边走去，想看建筑物的损毁情况，看是否有人需要帮助。和往常一样，他们边走边找 "阿克阿克" 弹壳。"阿克阿克" 弹壳这个名字模拟防空机枪的声音，这种弹壳是孩子们的宝贝。所有的男孩子都想得到这种弹壳，不管是用来收藏还是换其他小宝贝。两人走近炸弹爆炸处时，闻到了木头烧着的气味。再走着走着，脚下每一步都会踩到碎玻璃，发出咯喳咯喳声。

很难让人相信，这就是过去那个社区，那个他们长大后就一直在外玩耍的社区。闪电战之前，哈克尼的社区忙碌而友好。街边的房子安然挤在一起，房子之间靠得很近，都没有侧院和前院，只有后院和人行道。

and sidewalks. Harold had spent the first nine years of his life walking, running, and playing on the sidewalks and in his own and his friends' backyards.

Before the war, the only strong smell in the air came from the soap factories nearby. There were grocer's shops, tailor shops, and barber shops. Street musicians, with their violins or trumpets, played music to get money from passersby. People sat in the little Italian cafes drinking coffee in the daytime and wine at night, arguing enthusiastically about politics at all hours. The railway yards not far off rattled with the many trains going by.

Harold's father, Jack Pinter, was a tailor. By working hard, he made a decent living for himself, for his wife Frances, who stayed home to do the house-keeping, and for their son. Jack and Frances were glad to be able to live comfortably in their three-story brick home. They didn't envy the wealthy, who had servants and lavish houses. They felt sorry for those who lived in poverty. Mostly, they were too busy to worry much about what other families had or didn't have. This happy, hardworking couple had been married four years when their son Harold was born on October 10, 1930.

He was an only child, but he had grandparents, aunts, uncles, and

哈罗德人生最初的九年都在这里行走、奔跑，在人行道上、自家和朋友家的后院里玩耍。

战争以前，空气中唯一浓烈的气味来自附近的肥皂厂。这里有杂货店、裁缝店和理发店。这里有街头音乐家，他们弹着小提琴，或者吹着喇叭，向路人要点小钱。人们坐在小小的意大利咖啡馆里，白天喝咖啡，晚上饮葡萄酒，总是热烈地讨论着政治问题。不远处的铁路上，有许多火车经过，铁轨嘻嘻嘻嘻响着。

哈罗德的父亲杰克·品特是个裁缝。通过辛勤劳动，他为自己、妻子弗朗西斯(家庭主妇)和儿子赚得了体面的生活。杰克和弗朗西斯很乐意住在他们的三层砖房里。他们不羡慕那些拥有仆人和奢侈房子的富人，很同情那些生活在贫困中的穷人。大多数时候，他们很忙，无暇顾及别的家庭的所有所无。1930年10月10日他们的儿子哈罗德出生，此时这对快乐、勤劳的夫妇已经结婚四年了。

哈罗德是家中独子，但他有祖父母、姨妈、舅舅和表兄弟姐妹，

cousins, all part of a big Jewish family living nearby. Three of his grandparents had come to London from Poland and one came from Russia. The members of this large family visited each other and celebrated most Jewish holidays with lively gatherings. Because Harold was surrounded by so many loving relatives, he didn't feel lonely. Besides, when he wanted children to play with, he made them up. At least he did before he started school and had real children to play with.

In his backyard, when he was only four or five years old, Harold played with his imaginary friends. There, and in the little neglected garden at the back of the house, he held lively conversations with children he invented. In a sense, he was a budding playwright at an early age. He made up exciting scenes in his head, though he was too young to write them down. He made up dialogues and spoke all the parts out loud. This early desire for company and the pleasure he got from using his imagination to satisfy that desire are tied to his later interest in playwriting.

Inside his house on Thistlewaite Road in Hackney before the war, Harold's imaginary world wasn't limited to imaginary friends and their adventures. By the time he was six, he could read. He read

这个犹太大家庭的所有成员都住得很近。他的祖父母中三位从波兰来到伦敦，一位来自俄罗斯。这个大家庭的成员相互拜访，通过活泼、热烈的聚会，一起庆祝大多数犹太节日。由于哈罗德周围有这么多至亲，他并不感到孤单。再者，想要玩伴时，他会自己想象出来。他上学后才有真正的玩伴，在这以前，他都是靠这些想象的玩伴来陪伴的。

哈罗德才四五岁时，就在自家后院和想象中的朋友玩耍。在屋后那乏人问津的花园里，他和自己想象的孩子活泼地交谈。某种意义上说，他幼年时期就是剧坛新秀了。他在脑中设想激动的场景，不过那时他还小，没将这些写下来。他编出对话，并大声念出来。他很早就靠想象来寻求玩伴，靠想象的玩伴得到快乐，这些都与他后来对戏剧创作的兴趣密不可分。

战争以前，在哈克尼希斯尔韦特路的家里，哈罗德想象的世界并不局限于这些虚构的朋友及其遭遇。六岁时，他就能够自己阅读了。他读

fairy tales and folk tales about dwarves, trolls[1], witches, and leprechauns[2]. He read Jewish tales of the golem[3], a man-made creature who came to life. When he was seven or eight years old, like many children, he began to write some stories of his own. His proud parents, in keeping with traditional Jewish values, encouraged their son with praise for his love of reading and writing, as well as for his wonderful imagination.

In 1939, when Winston Churchill, prime minister of England, announced that the country had declared war against Germany, Harold's life changed drastically. Before he suffered through the London blitz, he suffered through something that, for him, was almost as bad.

1. troll: *n.* (北欧传说中的) 侏儒
2. leprechaun: *n.* (爱尔兰传说中的) 小妖精
3. golem: *n.* (犹太传说中的) 有生命的泥人

关于小矮人、北欧侏儒、女巫、妖精的童话故事和民间传说。他读犹太民族传说中关于泥人(一种有生命的假人)的故事。七八岁时，和许多孩子一样，他开始自己写故事。哈罗德的父母很为此骄傲，他们依照犹太民族的传统价值观，用表扬来鼓励儿子对阅读和写作的热爱，以及他那奇妙的想象力。

1939年，英国首相温斯顿·丘吉尔对德国宣战。此时，哈罗德的生活发生了急剧变化。在遭遇伦敦闪电战之前，他遇到了一些同样不快的事。

Chapter Two

CAERHAYS CASTLE[1]

卡尔海斯城堡

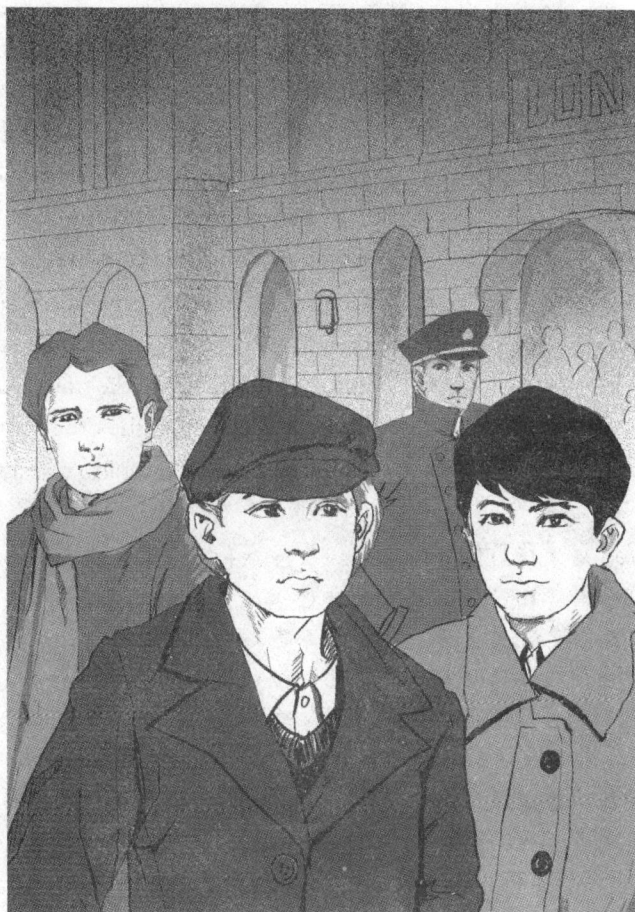

1. Caerhays Castle: 卡尔海斯城堡，由约翰·纳什于19世纪初设计，城堡因花园中的山茶花和杜鹃花而举世闻名

*H*arold stood in line to be checked for head lice[1]. As the woman in white bent his head this way and that, combing through his dark hair and peering at his scalp[2], he tried to keep from crying. He knew England was going into a war with Germany, but he wasn't sad about that. He didn't really have a clear idea of what it meant to go to war. He didn't know what it meant to be under attack. He certainly didn't know that in a year he would be crouching in a Morrison shelter with his mother and father. All he knew was that he was being sent away from his home. He was too old to think — as some of the smaller children did — that he was sent away from home because he had been naughty[3]. Nevertheless, he was miserable. He didn't want to leave his mother and father.

"Don't worry, dear," his mother reassured him, "we'll come to visit you just as soon as we can."

Harold just looked up at his mother without saying anything. He couldn't say much in response. All of the fear and sorrow that he and the other children felt, all of the commotion[4] in the railway station, and the rush to board the train made him unusually quiet. Besides, with the other boys from school so close by[5], he didn't want to take a chance on talking.

1. lice: *n.* (单数形式为 louse) 虱子
2. scalp: *n.* 头皮
3. naughty: *adj.* 顽皮的，淘气的
4. commotion: *n.* 喧闹，混乱的局面
5. close by: *adv.* 在附近，在旁边

哈罗德排队等候检查，看头上长没长虱子。身穿白大褂的女医生把他的头歪向这边，又歪向那边，梳着他的棕黑色头发，盯着他的头皮，他强忍着没哭出来。他知道英国与德国正在打仗，但他并不悲伤。他并不明白战争意味着什么，也不懂遭受袭击意味着什么。他显然不知道，一年以后，他会和父母蜷缩在莫里森防空掩体里。他只知道要被送出家门。许多更小的孩子遇到这种情况，会认为自己被送出家是因为太淘气，哈罗德已经过了这个年龄，不会这么想。不过，他还是难过不已。他不想离开父母。

"别担心，亲爱的，"哈罗德的母亲向他保证，"我们会尽快来看你。"

哈罗德抬头看着母亲，一声不吭。他无法用言语来回答。他和其他孩子所感受到的一切恐惧和悲伤，火车站台上的拥挤，挤上火车的匆忙，都让他异乎寻常的平静。此外，学校里其他男孩子和他靠得这么近，他

He was so close to tears he might break down.

As he climbed aboard the train, he turned back for one last look at his parents. Neither he, his parents, nor any of the other children or their parents knew where the train would take them. Inside the passenger car, he took a seat beside one of his friends from school.

The British government had decided to get children out of harm's way[1] when it had become clear that the German air force was going to attack London. Hundreds of children from the city were sent to different parts of England. This evacuation[2] of children from London took place in only three days. It began on September 2, 1939, the day before the British Prime Minister announced over the radio on the morning of September 3, that Britain was declaring war on Germany. Millions of children were rushed to railway stations. Mothers with infant children were also evacuated. Each child carried only a few belongings. This 1939 evacuation was the fastest and largest movement of human beings in history. The process was orderly, but the atmosphere was chaotic.

Lulled[3] by the rhythmic clacking of the train's wheels, Harold felt calmer. He caught glimpses of the city getting farther and farther behind as his train

1. out of harm's way: 脱离危险，免受伤害
2. evacuation: n. 撤离，疏散
3. lull: v. 使平静，使情绪和缓

什么也不想缩。他差点忍不住要哭出来。

爬上火车，他转身看了父母最后一眼。他、他的父母，其他孩子及其父母都不知道火车将把他们带往何处。在车厢里，他挨在同校一个好友边上坐了下来。

当有明显迹象表明德国空军要袭击伦敦时，英国政府决定将孩子们转移到安全的地方。伦敦成千上万的孩子们被送往英国各地。从伦敦疏散孩子的工作仅用了三天。疏散从1939年9月2日开始，次日晨，英国首相通过广播宣布英国对德国宣战。疏散当中，成千上万的孩子们被匆匆送往各火车站。带着婴儿的母亲也在疏散之列。每个孩子只带了少许随身行李。1939年的疏散是人类历史上规模最大、行动最为迅速的疏散。整个过程秩序井然，但气氛显得十分混乱。

火车轮毂有节奏的咣啷咣啷声使哈罗德冷静了下来。火车快速驶离伦

sped away from London. He and the other boys began to talk and even laugh occasionally as they rode through the English countryside.

After a few hours, they were told to gather their belongings. They had reached their destination. The porter[1] stood beside the door as the boys climbed down the steps onto the platform. Harold and the other boys from his Hackney neighborhood read the station sign that said "Mevagissey".

"Cornwall[2]", one boy said out loud. Mevagissey is a town in Cornwall, and their new temporary home was about five miles away from the town.

The twenty-four boys, aged five to twelve, got into motor cars waiting to drive them away. A few minutes later, topping a little hill, the boys in the car Harold rode in let out a gasp. There in the valley was a huge castle. It looked like a castle from the Middle Ages. The boys could imagine knights riding out of it on their big war horses, ready for battle.

In Cornwall, where he stayed for a year, Harold ate in the castle and slept in the stable. He learned that Caerhays Castle isn't a real castle. It wasn't built in feudal[3] times. It was built in 1808. Designed by

---

1. porter: *n.* 列车员
2. Cornwall: 康沃尔郡，位于英国西南部的一个郡
3. feudal: *adj.* 封建的，封建制的

敦，哈罗德看着城市越来越远的影子。火车驶过英国乡村时，他开始和其他男孩说话，甚至偶尔发出笑声。

几小时之后，有人叫大家拿好行李。他们已到达目的地。列车员站在门旁，孩子们爬下火车，上了站台。哈罗德和其他哈克尼街区的男孩看见车站站牌上写着"梅瓦吉西"。

"康沃尔，"一个男孩大声说道。梅瓦吉西是康沃尔郡的一个小镇，他们的临时新家离小镇大约五英里。

这24个年龄在5至12岁之间的男孩爬上汽车等待出发。几分钟后，在一座小山顶上，和哈罗德同一辆车的男孩们齐声惊叹。山谷处有座巨大的城堡，仿佛来自中世纪。孩子们可以想象骑士骑着高大的战马，扬鞭离开城堡，欲投入战斗的模样。

哈罗德在康沃尔郡住了一年。他在城堡中吃，在马厩里住。他得知卡尔海斯城堡并不是真正的城堡，并非建于封建时代，而是1808年由名

John Nash, a fashionable architect, it was meant to look like a medieval[1] castle.

Today, the spectacular Caerhays Castle still nestles among the trees in a pretty valley near the rugged coast of Cornwall, in southwestern England. The large, turreted[2] building is still surrounded by sweet-smelling magnolia[3] trees and camellia[4] bushes brought from China in the early 1900s.

The scenery of their new home was quite different than what Harold and the other boys from Hackney Elementary School had grown up with. They were used to the bustling sidewalks of Lower Clapton Road in their London neighborhood, with its constant noise of motorcars and workers. In their home in Cornwall, birds chirping[5] nearby and the sound of the sea not far away were at times the loudest sounds from outside the stable, where the boys slept in bunk beds[6]. Cattle grazed on the peaceful hillsides.

Life for the boys wasn't peaceful, however. Their teacher had come with them from London. He was strict. Sometimes he was mean. The boys didn't like him much and called him "Fat Nelly"

1. medieval: *adj.* 中古的，中世纪的

2. turreted: *adj.* 有尖塔的，塔状的

3. magnolia: *n.* 木兰，木兰花

4. camellia: *n.* 山茶，山茶花

5. chirp: *v.* (形容鸟类的) 鸣叫，叽叽喳喳

6. bunk bed: *n.* 能睡两或三人，通常带有扶梯的床铺；上下铺

嘭一时的建筑师约翰·纳什仿照中世纪城堡的样式设计的。

如今，壮观的卡尔海斯城堡依然依偎在漂亮山谷的树丛中，靠近位于英国西南角康沃尔郡崎岖的海岸。带角楼的巨大建筑仍旧为香气四溢的木兰和山茶所围绕。这些花是 20 世纪初从中国引进的。

他们这个新家的景色，和哈罗德以及其他哈克尼小学同学成长的环境大不相同。他们习惯了伦敦社区下克勒普顿路拥挤的街道，也习惯了那儿汽车的噪音和工人的喧闹。而在康沃尔郡的家里，孩子们睡在马厩的上下铺上，有时候近处小鸟的叽喳和不远处大海的涛声就是马厩外传来的最大声响了。附近的牛羊在山坡上安静地吃草。

不过，生活对男孩们来说并不平静。他们的老师也一道从伦敦来到这里。他十分严厉，有时比较凶。男孩们不怎么喜欢他，私下里叫他"胖

behind his back. Often the boys themselves were mean. Their homesickness and fear for their families in London made them angry, and they took out their anger on each other.

Despite the beauty around them, they couldn't forget the war. Once, they saw a group of the new British spitfire airplanes[1] flying overhead. That sight thrilled them. They were all proud of the spitfires. These one-seater fighter planes manufactured to shoot down German bombers and fighter planes could twist and turn quickly in the air. They could dive and climb with ease in battles thousands of feet above the ground. Many of the boys daydreamed about being fighter pilots and helping to save their country from the Germans.

Harold would like to have seen a spitfire shooting down a German plane. He enjoyed talking about the different planes, though he wasn't as fascinated[2] by them as some of the other boys, who read and talked about them almost constantly.

In the daytime during the week, Harold could distract[3] himself from loneliness and fear with his work and play at school. The boys studied at the village school, walking there every week-day morning from the castle.

1. spitfire airplane: *n.* 喷火式战斗机，是二战期间广泛为英军和盟军使用的单座战斗机
2. fascinate: *v.* 入迷，着迷
   be fascinated by: 为…所深深吸引
3. distract: *v.* (注意力等的)转移，分散

内利"。男孩们自己也常使坏。他们想家，担心伦敦的家人出事，这些心思闹得他们脾气暴躁，大家互相拿对方出气。

尽管周围环境很美，但孩子们忘不了战争。曾有一次，他们看见一群新式英国喷火式战斗机飞过头顶。这个景象让他们十分兴奋。他们为喷火式飞机感到骄傲。这种单座战斗机是为击落德国轰炸机和战斗机而造，能在空中迅速旋转、翻跟头。作战中，它们能在距地面几千英尺的高空轻松俯冲和爬升。许多男孩梦想成为战斗机飞行员，参加祖国的抗德战斗。

哈罗德很想看到喷火式战斗机击落德军飞机。他喜欢谈论不同的飞机，不过他不像某些男孩对飞机那样痴迷，这些男孩子几乎总是在看飞机的资料，没事就谈论这些飞机。

一周里面，哈罗德白天靠在学校学习和玩耍来排遣孤独和恐惧。男孩们在村中的学校上学，每天早晨从城堡走去学校。

Lying in his hard little bunk at night, Harold tossed and turned[1]. The bunk was too narrow. He rolled onto his left side then his right. He lay on his back awhile. Then he lay on his stomach. No matter how he lay, he couldn't get comfortable. He had trouble falling asleep. He pulled the blanket up over him. The drafty[2] stable was cold in the wintertime. He was keenly aware of the other boys around him in their own bunks. He could hear some of them tossing and turning, too, trying to get to sleep. One or two boys snored[3]. Another cried out softly in his sleep. Through many lonely hours, Harold lay awake. Night time was the time he missed his parents most of all. They couldn't afford to pay for train tickets to visit him very often. When they did come, their visits seemed too short.

On one visit, his parents took a picture of him, sitting on the root of a big tree near the castle. Harold smiled for the photograph, but his smile didn't hide the serious-ness of his face. Though he was glad his parents were with him, he knew they would be leaving soon. The family's good-bye at the end of that day's visit was, as always, upsetting for all of them. Mother, father, and child hugged each other tightly.

1. toss and turn: 翻来覆去，辗转反侧
2. drafty: *adj.* 通风的，漏风的
3. snore: *v.* 打鼾，打呼噜

晚上，躺在窄小的硬床铺上，哈罗德辗转反侧。床铺太窄了。他一会儿往左翻，一会儿往右翻，一会儿平躺，一会儿又趴着睡。不论怎么躺，总也不舒服。他失眠了。他把毯子拉起来裹住头。冬天，透风的马厩很冷。他能敏锐地感受到周围床上其他男孩的动静，听到其他人也在翻来覆去，试着入睡。一两个男孩打着呼噜，另一个在梦中哭了。很多孤独长夜里，哈罗德都躺在那里睡不着。夜晚时分，他最想念父母。他们付不起火车票钱，没法常来看他，而当父母来看他时，见面又是那么短暂。

有一次见面时，哈罗德的父母给他照了张相。哈罗德坐在城堡附近的一棵大树根上，摆出笑容，但笑容无法掩饰他心情的沉重。他很高兴能和父母在一起，但他知道他们不久就会离去。那天探访结束时，一家人的互相道别还是一样让每个人伤感。临别前，父母和孩子紧紧拥抱。

After one such good-bye, instead of walking back to the castle, Harold stood outside it and turned around. On the road far away he saw his mother and father walking away, impossibly small. His chest tightened with unshed[1] tears. Without thinking, he began to run toward his departing parents. He was a strong runner, and he covered the distance between them quickly. As he got closer, he called to them to stop. They turned, hearing his cries. His mother held out her arms. He ran into them, and she held him close. His father reached out[2] and lovingly smoothed Harold's dark hair. The three of them wished they could stay like this. Still, Harold knew his parents had to catch their train back to London. After a few minutes, he had to tell them good-bye again.

Harold didn't want to be safe when his parents were in danger. What if they died, as his friend's parents had? A bomb could hit their home at any time. The choice wasn't his, however. Nor was it his parents' choice. The government had insisted that children be evacuated.

As it turned out, Harold wasn't safe for long. Ironically[3], the government allowed him and many

1. unshed: *adj.* 没有流出的(常指眼泪)
2. reach out: 伸出双手，多指提供帮助
   如: We must *reach out* to those in need. 我们应该伸出援手，帮助有困难的人。
3. ironically: *adv.* 具有讽刺意味，用反语或讽刺的方式

一次道别后，哈罗德没有走回城堡，而是在城堡之外，转过身来。远处的路上，他看见远去的父母，背影是那么渺小。他强忍眼泪，感到胸口发紧。他来不及想，就朝离去的父母跑去。他跑得很快，不久就赶上了他们。快追到时，他叫他们停下。父母转过身，听到了他的哭声。母亲张开手臂，他跑向她，母亲紧紧抱住他，父亲也伸出手，满怀关爱地抚摸着哈罗德棕黑色的头发。三个人多想能这样在一起，不过，哈罗德知道父母得赶火车返回伦敦。几分钟后，他又不得不再次和他们道别。

父母身处危险，哈罗德也不愿独享太平。若是像他朋友一样，他的父母也都死了怎么办？炸弹随时会炸到他们家。不过，他可没法选择，他的父母也没法选择，是政府坚持要疏散儿童。

果然，哈罗德的太平日子没过多久。具有讽刺意味的是，就在最危

of the other children to return to London just when the danger became greatest. The Germans didn't attack London much during the time Harold and the other Hackney Grammar School children were in Cornwall. They were allowed to return to their parents in London because the expected attacks hadn't come. However, not long after the children got back to their homes in the city, the Nazis began bombing in full force.

险的时候，政府允许了他和许多其他孩子返回伦敦。哈罗德和哈克尼文法小学的同学在康沃尔时，德军并未大规模袭击伦敦。由于预料的袭击没有到来，孩子们获准回到了父母身边。不过，等孩子们返回城里家中不久，纳粹的全面轰炸就开始了。

Chapter Three

MORE BOMBS

战火延续

In spite of the danger, Harold was glad to be back in London. He sometimes missed walking along the rugged coast near Caerhays Castle, but London was his home. He wanted to be with his parents, not four hundred miles away from them. However, now, with the floor shaking under his feet, he thought of the peaceful rolling hills and the quiet of Cornwall. Another bomb exploded outside.

"That one was close," Harold's mother Frances said.

"We should've gone to the underground," Jack, Harold's father replied.

Like many other Londoners, the Pinters hated to go to one of the city's many public shelters. They even hated to climb into their own little Morrison shelter. It felt cowardly. It felt braver — even if foolish — to refuse to hide from the bombs.

Looking out from behind the heavy black curtain over the window, Harold saw pink lights flashing on the horizon. The pink lights were from the many fires caused by incendiary[1] bombs.

Incendiary bombs were small. Their only purpose was to start fires. The light of these fires helped

---

1. incendiary: *adj.* 纵火的，煽动的
   incendiary bombs: 燃烧弹

尽管危险尚存，哈罗德仍很高兴能回到伦敦。他有时会想念在卡尔海斯城堡附近的崎岖海岸上漫步的感觉，但毕竟伦敦才是他的家。他想和父母在一起，而不是距离他们400英里之遥。不过现在，随着脚下地板的震动，他又怀念起康沃尔那些起伏绵延的小丘和那里的宁静来。又一枚炸弹在外面爆炸了。

"这回够近的，"哈罗德的母亲弗朗西斯说道。

"我们该躲到地下去。"哈罗德的父亲杰克回答说。

伦敦公共防空洞不少，但和许多伦敦人一样，品特一家厌恶去防空洞。他们甚至讨厌爬进自家狭窄的莫里森防空掩体里去。躲进防空洞的行为让他们觉得懦弱。不去躲这些炸弹，才会显得勇敢，哪怕这样做有些愚蠢。

透过厚厚的黑窗帘向窗户外望去，哈罗德见到地平线上有粉红色的光在闪耀。这些粉红色的光是由燃烧弹引起的许多场大火发出的。

燃烧弹很小，唯一的用途是点火。火光可以帮助德军飞行员发现城

German pilots find their targets in the city.

The high explosive bombs[1] were big. Harold knew that the German Stuka airplane[2] could carry a thousand-pound bomb. The larger bomber airplane, the Heinkel[3], could carry much heavier bomb loads. The terrible fire-power delivered by these planes had never been dropped on a city before.

It was November, 1940. London had been under attack since September.

"Well, there's no place safe if the palace can be bombed," said Harold almost to himself, as he stood at the window.

"Nothing sacred about the palace," his mother commented. Frances hadn't thought it was such important news last September 13th that the King and Queen of England had almost been killed by the first bomb strike on Buckingham Palace[4].

"The life of any man's worth is as much as the life of a king," she continued. Frances'

1. high explosive bomb: n. 高爆炸弹
2. Stuka airplane: n. 斯图卡轰炸机，二战期间德军的俯冲式轰炸机
3. Heinkel: n. 二战期间德国空军使用最多的主战轰炸机
4. Buckingham Palace: 白金汉宫，是英国皇室在伦敦的官方住所，位于威斯敏斯特城内，是主持国家事务和皇家宴会的重要场所，亦是一处旅游名胜，在国家欢庆和危险时期还是英国人民的集会地点

市里的目标。

高爆炸弹则很大。哈罗德知道德国斯图卡轰炸机能携带1000磅的炸弹。体型更大的亨克尔轰炸机的载弹量更大。这些飞机在城市上空投下了数量空前的火力。

这时是1940年11月。伦敦从9月份起就一直遭受空袭。

"如果王宫都遭受袭击的话，那么就毫无安全之处了，"哈罗德站在窗户边，几乎是在自言自语。

"王宫也不是什么圣地，"他母亲评价说。9月13日，英国国王和王后差点被第一枚投到白金汉宫的炸弹炸死，但弗朗西斯不觉这是什么重大新闻。

"任何人的生命都与国王的生命价值相等，"她继续说着。弗朗西斯这种大不敬的观点显示出她伦敦东区的出身。她并不喜欢所有关于皇室

irreverent[1] opinions showed her Cockney[2] background. She didn't like all the talk about the royal couple's bravery. They were no braver than most Londoners, as far as she could see. And they had a greater duty to be brave anyway.

Harold smiled to himself. He liked his mother's attitude. Harold's family hadn't been one of those that rushed out on that afternoon of September 13 to see the King and Queen on a visit to the East End. Reporters had praised the pluck[3] of the royal couple to come out after being bombed that same morning.

"You sound like my brother," Jack said to his wife. Jack's brother was a communist. He and Jack argued often about politics. Jack was more religious than political. Much of Jack's thought reflected his Jewish faith.

Frances and Jack argued partly because they were tired of the bombing. Months of daily bomb attacks had worn on their nerves[4]. Several times they'd had to evacuate with their son Harold. At first they'd fussed at him for always carrying his cricket bat with him when they left the house to go

---

1. irreverent: *adj.* 不尊敬的
2. Cockney: 伦敦东区，伦敦东部、港口附近的地区，曾是拥挤的贫民区，街道狭窄、房屋稠密，多为19世纪中期建筑。二战期间，伦敦东区大部分遭受轰炸破坏，后重建，是伦敦传统工业区，有服装、制鞋、家具、印刷、卷烟、食品等工业。
3. pluck: *n.* 勇气
4. wear on their nerves: 使某人精神紧张，令某人难以忍受

夫妇英勇无畏的说法。她认为他们并不比大多数伦敦人勇敢，而且他们有责任要表现得更勇敢无畏。

哈罗德兀自一笑。他欣赏母亲的态度。9月13日下午，英国国王和王后来视察伦敦东区，哈罗德一家并没有挤着去看。记者曾称赞皇室夫妇在早晨同样受袭后仍照旧出来视察的勇气。

"你这口气像我弟弟，"杰克对妻子说。杰克的弟弟是共产党员，他和杰克常为政治话题争执不下。杰克信奉宗教而非政治，许多观念反映出他的犹太教信仰。

弗朗西斯和杰克之所以争论，部分原因是他们都厌倦了轰炸。持续数月的每日轰炸折磨着他们的神经。好几次他们必须和哈罗德一起撤离。最初他们对哈罗德离开家去防空洞时总带着板球棒感到奇怪。

to a shelter. It was crowded there, but his bat didn't take up much room. Besides, they knew that for him it was a comfort to have the bat with him. He loved sports. His bat was a prized possession. He knew looters[1] often stole from bombed houses. Besides taking his bat with him meant that maybe he would live to play cricket again.

Harold was glad they weren't in a shelter tonight. He was sick of air shelters. He didn't like the crowd there. Many people took shelter from the bombs by hurrying to underground rail stations. Many took shelter in school buildings or churches. Some people had the buried Anderson shelters[2] that they could enter from their own yards. Some, like Harold's family, had Morrison shelters inside their homes.

The blast of explosions came every few minutes. The sound of anti-aircraft guns cracked continuously. Harold could hear fire trucks carrying firemen to turn their water hoses on the burning buildings in the East End. He didn't mind the noise of the attacks so much. He minded more the silence before the attacks. Too often he'd sat with others, huddled down in shelters waiting for the drone of airplane engines.

1. looter: *n.* 掠夺者，抢劫者
2. Anderson shelters: *n.* 二战期间英国政府向公民派发的防空掩体，由威廉·帕特森和奥斯卡·克里森设计，与莫里森防空掩体不同，常埋在户外地下

防空洞里很挤，好在板球棒也不怎么占地方。此外，他们知道带着球棒对哈罗德也是个安慰。他热爱体育运动。他的球棒是件奖品。他知道会有抢劫者抢劫遭受轰炸的房子。另外，带上球棒对他来说或许意味着自己仍会活下去，可以继续打板球。

哈罗德很高兴今晚不用呆在防空洞里。他不喜欢防空掩体，不喜欢那里拥挤的人群。许多人匆匆挤进地铁来躲避轰炸。许多人躲进学校或教堂的建筑物里。有些人在院子里埋了安德森防空掩体，可从自家后院进去。有些人，如同哈罗德家一样，呆在房内的莫里森防空掩体里。

爆炸的冲击波几分钟就袭来一阵。防空机枪的声音响个不停。哈罗德听见载着消防员的救火车驶向东区燃烧起火的建筑，打开消防水龙头灭火。他并不在意空袭的噪音，他在意的是空袭前的寂静。他经常和别人一起挤在防空洞里，等待飞机引擎的嗡嗡声。

He moved the curtain a little more to the side. Frances had turned off the light in their living room, so no light showed when Harold opened the curtain.

Harold had been back a long time now, from Caerhays Castle, where he'd spent the "phony war". From September 1939 when thousands of children were evacuated until September 1940, the Londoners had expected attacks that mostly didn't come. Only a few weeks after their children had gone away, some mothers brought their children back to the city. As the months wore on and no big attack came, more and more children came back home. Harold was one of the last to return. He remembered how homesick he'd been. He resented being away. He begged his parents to come and take him home. At last they agreed. They thought maybe the report of a big attack would never come. They wanted their son back.

"The city is pretty by moonlight," wrote his mother in a letter telling Harold that maybe he could come home soon. Frances was beginning to get used to living with the blackouts at night.

Harold wished he'd never gone away. He hated to have missed any of the excitement. He wished he could've seen the barrage balloons[1] before they were painted a dingy[2] green. His mother said that when

1. barrage balloons: *n.* (军事的) 防空气球，阻塞气球
2. dingy: *adj.* 暗黑的

他把窗帘稍微拉向一边。弗朗西斯已经关掉了起居室的灯，因此当哈罗德拉开窗帘时不会漏出灯光。

哈罗德从卡尔海斯城堡回到家已经很久了，在那儿他躲过了"假的战争"。从1939年9月成千上万孩子们被疏散，到1940年9月，伦敦人预期的空袭大都没有发生。孩子们离开后才几周，有的母亲就把孩子接回城里。好几个月过去了，都没有大的空袭来临。于是，越来越多的孩子回到了家。哈罗德是最后一批回家的。他记得他是多么想家，他讨厌离家在外，恳求父母带他回家，他们最终答应了。他们想或许不会有大轰炸的消息了。他们也想要儿子回家。

"月光下的城市很美，"母亲在一封信里告诉哈罗德，也许他不久就能回家了。弗朗西斯开始习惯灯火管制后的夜晚。

哈罗德但愿当初就没有离开过。他讨厌错过任何激动人心的事情。

they were first put up, they were silver and looked magical up there in the sky. The big balloons, or blimps[1], were about sixty feet long and twenty-five feet wide. These tethered blimps floated at about five thousand feet. They were there to force the German bombers to have to fly high to avoid them and the cables that tethered[2] them. The higher the bombers flew, the less accurate their bombs.

He'd also missed the pleasures of the city. There were so many things to do that he couldn't do in the country. He could go to the movies again, now that he was back in London.

Not all the movie theaters were open, but some of them were. The longest running movie in London during the war was the American film *Gone with the Wind*[3].

Gone with the Wind is about the Civil War in the United States. The star of this movie, Vivien Leigh[4], was a popular British actress. She plays Scarlet O'Hara[5], a pretty, but spoiled southern belle who bravely faces the terrors of war. This movie was very popular with the Londoners, whose city was under

1. blimp: *n.* 小型飞艇
2. tether: *v.* （用绳索）拴着，系着
3. *Gone with the Wind*: 《乱世佳人》（又译《飘》），改编自美国女作家玛格丽特·米切尔1936年的小说《飘》，讲述了美国南北战争期间和战后南方重建背景下，女主角斯佳丽·奥哈拉的传奇生活。1939年由维克多·弗莱明执导，主要演员包括影星克拉克·盖博、费雯·丽、奥利维娅·德哈维兰等，电影《乱世佳人》获第12届奥斯卡最佳影片奖
4. Vivien Leigh: 费雯·丽（1913－1967），英国著名女演员，天生丽质，因在电影《乱世佳人》和《欲望号街车》中的出色表演而两度获得奥斯卡最佳女演员奖
5. Scarlet O'Hara: 斯佳丽·奥哈拉，《乱世佳人》中的女主角

他希望能在防空气球被涂成暗绿色前见到它们。母亲说，这些气球刚被放起来的时候是银白色的，在天空中仿佛有魔力一般。这些大型气球，或者叫做小型飞艇，约60英尺长、25英尺宽。这些拴在地面的小型飞艇漂浮在距地面5000英尺的空中，迫使德军轰炸机飞得更高，以避开飞艇和拴飞艇的绳索。轰炸机飞得越高，炸弹的精确度就越低。

哈罗德也怀念城里的乐趣。城里有许多乡下不能做的事情。现在回到伦敦，他又能去电影院了。

虽然并非所有的电影院都营业，但仍有一些营业的。战争期间，伦敦放映时间最长的是美国电影《乱世佳人》。

《乱世佳人》是部关于美国内战的电影。电影明星费雯·丽是位很受欢迎的英国女演员。她扮演的斯佳丽·奥哈拉是位漂亮、爱宠爱的南方

attack. They thought of their own fires when they saw the portrayal[1] of the burning of Atlanta, Georgia. They knew what it was to have invaders burn your city. They thought of their own efforts to keep up their spirits when they saw Scarlet's high-spirited efforts to survive. Londoners sat in the darkened theater and sympathized with this lovely survivor of a war that took place across the Atlantic Ocean nearly a century before World War II started. Many of them went to see the movie over and over again.

Harold wasn't so interested in *Gone with the Wind*. To a ten-year-old boy like him, only the battles and fires were exciting. Too much of the movie was a love story. But he liked going to movies with his friends. What was showing didn't much matter.

Harold closed the curtain. It was late. Time to go upstairs to bed. He had learned to sleep through the bombings.

The next evening, the Pinters had to evacuate their home. An even worse bomb attack was expected. Harold opened the back door to leave with his parents. Clutching[2] his cricket bat, he looked

1. portrayal: *n.* 描绘；描写；饰演
2. clutch: *v.* 紧握着，紧紧抓住

美女，她勇敢地面对战争所带来的恐惧。这部电影在处于空袭下的伦敦人中很受欢迎。他们看到佐治亚州亚特兰大市遭受火灾的景象，就想起伦敦城里的大火。他们对入侵者烧掉城市的行为感同身受。他们看到斯佳丽要活下去的那股斗志，就想自己也要努力保持抖擞精神。伦敦的人们坐在黑暗的剧院里，看着二战开始大约一个世纪前发生在大西洋彼岸的战争，同情着战争中那位可爱的幸存者。许多人都忍不住一遍又一遍地看这部电影。

哈罗德并不迷恋《乱世佳人》，对他这个10岁的男孩子来说，只有战争和大火才刺激，而这部电影大部分是爱情故事。但是他喜欢和朋友一起去电影院，放映什么并不重要。

哈罗德拉上窗帘。太晚了，该上楼睡觉去了。他已经学会在轰炸中入睡。

第二天早晨，品特一家必须离家疏散。一场更为猛烈的轰炸即将到

around. The backyard garden beyond the lilac[1] tree and the laundry behind the garden was already alight with fire. He hoped they'd have a home to come back to.

来。哈罗德打开后门，与父母亲一起离开家。他手中紧握板球棒，四处张望。后院花园外的丁香花树和花园后的洗衣房已经着火了。他希望回家时房子还在。

Chapter Four

OLD WAR AND NEW WAYS

旧战争和新思维

From September until November, 1940, London was almost the only target of German bomb raids. During that time, the Germans dropped almost 30,000 high explosive bombs on the city. The Pinter family and their home survived those first fifty-seven days of bombing and the cold hard winter that followed them. In the spring of 1941, Hitler's Nazi air force turned its attention to Russia. But the war wasn't over for Londoners. The Germans didn't give up on their plan to conquer England. In mid-April and in May, three of the worst attacks on London took place. Harold and his parents got safely through these attacks as well. Though many Londoners' homes had been destroyed, their home still stood. It had survived the worst of the air raids.

The Pinters were lucky. During the "blitzkrieg" or "lightning war", over 40,000 Londoners were killed. Just collecting and burying the dead was a dismaying task. Thousands were left homeless.

The bombings were never again as heavy as in the fall of 1940 and the late spring of 1941. But, they still occurred often enough to disrupt life and cause destruction for the next three years. Harold was evacuated from London three more times before the war was over.

He was sent to Reading[1] in 1941. Frances, his

1. Reading: 英国英格兰南部城市，伯克郡首府，位于肯尼特河与泰晤士河交汇处

从1940年9月到11月，伦敦几乎是德军唯一的轰炸目标。在此期间，德军在城市上空投下接近3万颗高爆炸弹。品特一家和他们的房子躲过了最初57天的轰炸和随后寒冷难挨的冬天。1941年春，希特勒的纳粹空军将注意力转向俄国，但是战争对伦敦人来说并未结束。德国人仍未放弃征服英国的计划。4月中旬和5月，伦敦遭受了三次最为严重的空袭。哈罗德和父母在空袭中安然无恙。许多伦敦人的房屋被炸毁，但他们家却依然完好，躲过了最为猛烈的空袭。

品特一家是幸运的。"闪电战"期间，4万多伦敦人被炸死。给死者收尸、掩埋尸体的任务就让人十分愁烦。成千上万人无家可归。

轰炸再也不像1940年秋和1941年4月底那样猛烈了。不过，在接下来的三年里，轰炸仍时有发生，常会干扰生活，引起破坏。战争结束前，哈罗德又从伦敦被疏散了三次。

1941年，哈罗德和母亲弗朗西斯一起被疏散到雷了。母子俩人住在

mother was evacuated with him. The two lived in Reading with a factory worker and his family. Harold missed his friends, and he spent more time with books. He read every night by candlelight. Still, he didn't do well in school. He failed an important exam to get into high school. His father protested the failing score, and Harold later took the exam again.

In Reading, Harold continued to keep up with sports, as he would all his life. He went to football games every week. He was happier than when he'd been at Caerhays Castle in Cornwall, far away from both his mother and father.

Mother and son went back to London to visit Jack when they could. One day when Harold and his mother had come into London, he learned that the Germans had launched a new kind of bomb. He was used to the noise of the airplanes and the artillery[1] fire, even the explosions of big bombs. Now he heard a new sound from overhead. He heard what sounded like a flying sewing machine. It was a V1 rocket bomb[2]. What Harold heard was one of the first of the famous "buzz" bombs. Sometimes called

1. artillery: *n.* 火炮；大炮；炮兵
2. V1 rocket bomb：V1型火箭弹，二战期间德军研制的火箭弹，是早期的巡航导弹。1944年6月到1945年3月间被用来袭击伦敦和安特卫普等城市的人口聚居区

一位工人家中。哈罗德想念朋友们，他用更多的时间来读书。他每晚秉烛夜读。不过，他的学习成绩不是太好。高中入学的一门重要考试他没考及格。哈罗德的父亲对这门不及格的成绩表示不满，哈罗德后来又参加了补考。

在雷了，哈罗德继续从事体育运动，这个爱好他后来坚持了一辈子。他每周都去看足球比赛。他比在康沃尔郡卡尔海斯城堡时期高兴，那时候父母都离他很远。

哈罗德母子俩一有空就回伦敦看望父亲杰克。有一天当哈罗德和母亲回到伦敦时，得知德军在发射一种新型炸弹。他对飞机和大炮的噪音已经习以为常，甚至对炸弹的爆炸声也感到习惯了。现在他听到头顶上一种新的声音，像是缝纫机从空中飞过。这是V1型火箭弹的声音。哈罗德听到的是第一批"嗡嗡"炸弹的声音。这种著名的炸弹又称"狮叫"，

"doodle-bugs[1]", these bombs seemed clumsy, almost funny. However, they were deadly.

Self-propelled[2] and set on a timer, when the buzz bomb's engine stopped, the bomb fell to the ground and exploded. In a way, this rocket was the first guided missile. It was set to fly for a certain amount of time. When that time was up, it would be over a certain bomb site.

For a while, Harold was evacuated to Leeds[3], Yorkshire. At Leeds, he saw the world famous cricket player, Len Hutton[4], play at Headingley Stadium. The young Harold was thrilled at the sight of this man's skill. He wanted to go up and speak to Hutton, but he was too shy. Nevertheless, he never forgot the experience. He said he "fell in love" with Hutton and remained passionate about the Yorkshire Cricket Club because of him.

By the time he was thirteen, he'd given up religious belief. He and his father often argued about Jewish law and traditions. Nevertheless, as a good Jewish boy he studied Hebrew and prepared for his bar mitzvah[5]. He was in London enough time to go

1. doodle-bug: *n.* 蜥蚁。英国口语中指"导弹"
2. propel: *v.* 推动; 推进; 激励。self-propelled, (导弹) 自我推进的
3. Leeds: 英国英格兰西约克郡的城市和都市区, 是英国伦敦以外最大的商业、金融和法律服务中心
4. Len Hutton: 莱恩·赫顿 (1916–1990), 英国著名板球运动员, 二战后主导英国和国际板球界十多年, 曾任英国国家板球队队长
5. mitzvah: *n.* (犹太教的) 戒律。bar mitzvah, 犹太宗教仪式, 犹太男孩女孩的宗教成年礼

它们看起来笨拙, 甚至有些滑稽。不过, 它们却是致命的。

嗡嗡炸弹是自我推进的, 设有定时器, 一旦引擎停止, 炸弹就会落地爆炸。从某种程度上说, 这种火箭弹是最早的导弹。它能设定一段飞行时间, 到了特定时间, 它就会飞到某个轰炸地点的上方。

哈罗德曾一度被疏散到约克郡的利兹。在利兹的黑了利体育馆, 他见到了世界著名板球运动员莱恩·赫顿。年轻的哈罗德为其球技迷住了。他想上前与赫顿攀谈, 但因过于害羞没去。尽管如此, 这却成为他难以忘怀的经历。他说他"爱上"赫顿了。因为赫顿, 哈罗德此后一直钟爱约克郡板球俱乐部。

哈罗德 13 岁时放弃了宗教信仰。他和父亲常常争论犹太教律法和传统。不过, 作为一个犹太好孩子, 他学习希伯来语, 为犹太受戒仪式

to a school near Lea Bridge to learn what he needed for this ritual marking his passage into manhood. However, Harold only went through this ritual because his parents insisted. His childhood had been disrupted by evacuations and bombings. Such troubles strengthened some people's religious faith. It didn't bolster Harold's faith. By the time he was twelve or thirteen years old, he had developed a critical nature. He questioned many of the beliefs of the adults around him. In fact, with money he got as gifts for his bar mitzvah, he bought a copy of the Irish novel, *Ulysses*, by James Joyce[1]. His father heartily disapproved of this purchase. The book's difficult style and sexual content caused the book to be banned in many places. That Harold wanted the book shows his early interest in going outside the conventional.

In 1944, near the end of the war, Harold was evacuated again. He went to rural Norfolk[2] with his schoolmates. He wasn't there long, but the place made a strong impression on him. He liked the countryside. Fifteen years later, he used his memory of a Norfolk house, with its garden and sweet-smelling honeysuckle, in his play, *A Slight Ache*.

1. James Joyce: 詹姆斯·乔伊斯 (1882–1941)，爱尔兰作家、诗人。主要作品包括《都柏林人》(*Dubliners*, 1914)、《一位青年艺术家的画像》(*A Portrait of the Artist as a Young Man*, 1916)、《尤利西斯》(*Ulysses*, 1922) 和《芬尼根守灵》(*Finnegans Wake*, 1939)，他运用意识流 (stream of consciousness) 手法开创了文学的新领域
2. Norfolk: 诺福克郡, 位于英格兰东部

做准备。由于常在伦敦，他还在伦敦利桥附近一所学校学习宗教习俗，为标志着他进入成年的受戒仪式做准备。不过，哈罗德是在父母的坚持下接受受戒仪式的。他的童年常受疏散和轰炸的干扰。这些遭遇增强了某些人的宗教信仰，但却没有增强哈罗德的信仰。哈罗德十二三岁时就养成了质疑的习惯。他质疑身边成年人的很多信仰。其实，他用受戒礼上获得的礼金买了本爱尔兰小说：詹姆斯·乔伊斯的《尤利西斯》。他父亲完全不赞成买这本书。因风格晦涩，性描写过多，此书在不少地方被列为禁书。哈罗德买这本书，表明他很早就有超脱传统的兴趣。

1944 年战争结束前，哈罗德再一次被疏散。他和同学一起去偏远的诺福克郡。他在那儿呆得不长，但那里给他留下了深刻的印象。他喜爱乡村。15 年后，他将对诺福克郡一所房子的记忆，包括房子的花园和馨香的野金菊花，写进了戏剧《微痛》中。

Though the war was going on, when the city wasn't being bombed, and he was home in London, his life was mostly happy. His father was a steady worker, leaving home at seven o'clock in the morning and working until seven in the evening. His mother stayed home to cook and clean. Harold went to school on weekdays. He played with his friends after school and on weekends.

Sometimes Harold and his good friend Mick Goldstein played cricket together. They walked down to nearby open fields in the early morning on Sundays. Using a tree as a wicket, they took turns batting and bowling. Harold would remember those early morning practices with his friend not far from the Lea River as among the happiest times of his life.

Life went on for him pretty much as it did for children in big cities everywhere. Still, there was an air of recklessness, a strong sense that life was short. He later said that there was a new sexual charge to people's feelings because of the danger of the war. Many people felt the urge to "live for the moment". Old rules didn't seem so important. Women were freer to leave home than they'd been before the war. They went into the workforce in great numbers. They became bank cashiers and factory workers. They drove fire trucks and milk wagons. Though many men didn't like it, they had to tolerate women working outside

战争仍在继续，不过，当城市没有遭受轰炸，哈罗德在伦敦家里的时候，他的日子多半还是快乐的。父亲一直上班，早晨七点离家，晚上七点才回来。母亲在家做饭、打扫卫生。哈罗德平日上学，放学后和周末便同朋友们玩耍。

有时哈罗德和好朋友米克·戈尔茨坦一起打板球。星期天清晨，他们有时会走到附近的空场，用树做球门，两人轮流击球投球。哈罗德将清晨与朋友在利河边打板球的经历，当作一生中最为快乐的时光之一。

和其他大城市的男孩们一样，哈罗德的日子仍在继续着。不过，周遭有种肆无忌惮的气氛，有种生命短暂的强烈感觉。他后来说道，因为战争的危险，人们有种新的性兴奋。许多人强烈感到有必要"活在当下"。旧的规矩不再重要，女人可以比战争以前更自由地走出家门了。她们大批加入劳动大军，成为银行出纳和工厂工人，开起消防车和送奶车。尽

the home. Women felt a new energy. British and American servicemen[1] on leave filled the bars and restaurants. Relationships formed between women and men who might never have met except for the war.

Many people were homeless. Many mourned their dead family and friends. They worried about their fathers, sons, and husbands at the front. There were shortages of gasoline and some food items. Sugar was rationed as was butter, tea, margarine, and eggs during part of the war. All of these things were hard. People did what they could to forget their troubles.

During the summers, Londoners stayed in the city for the most part. They went to the zoo. They swam in the public swimming pools. Theaters for live performances provided entertainment for many. People went to plays, especially comedies and musicals, to lift their spirits.

One of the most popular songs of the war was "The White Cliffs of Dover", which expressed sentimental feelings about the white chalk cliffs on the coast of the English Channel near the city of Dover, England. Its popularity isn't surprising. These cliffs are at the nar-

1. servicemen : n. 军人

然很多男性不喜欢这种改变，但他们不得不接受女性出门上班的事实。女性感到了一种新的活力。英国和美国休假的军人挤在酒吧和餐馆里，男女之间生出各种关系。倘若不是战争，这些关系或许永远不会发生。

许多人无家可归，许多人哀悼死去的亲人和朋友。他们担心身处前线的父亲、孩子和丈夫。城里汽油和部分食品短缺。糖、黄油、茶叶、人造黄油和鸡蛋等都实行战时配给制。一切都很艰难，人们尽力忘却各自的烦恼。

夏天的时候，伦敦人大都呆在城里。他们去动物园，在公共游泳池里游泳，剧院的现场表演为许多人提供了娱乐。人们去看戏，特别是看喜剧和音乐剧，以此来振奋精神。

战争期间最流行的一首歌是《多佛海岸的白色峭壁》，歌曲表达了英格兰多佛市附近英吉利海峡边的白色峭壁所引发的感伤。它会受欢迎并不令人意外。这些悬崖在英吉利海峡最狭窄之处，轮船由此往来欧陆，

rowest part of the English Channel, where boats commonly cross to and from Europe. The cliffs are an important symbol. British people didn't seem to mind that the American songwriter Nick Burton, made a mistake in the lyrics. He wrote "There'll be bluebirds over the white cliffs of Dover," not knowing that bluebirds are American birds and not English ones. Bluebirds symbolize happiness in American story and song, and the British were willing to accept them as a promise that better times would return. British songwriter Hugh Charley wrote another of the most popular songs: "We'll Meet Again". Many families missed their husbands, sons, and fathers, off fighting the war. "We'll Meet Again" expressed the sentiment that these men would be reunited with their loved ones.

Harold wasn't given much to popular sentiments like those expressed in these popular songs. As a Jewish youngster, he didn't reject a cultural heritage that included a deep respect for argument, abstract ideas, and art. In wartime London, there was an upsurge in interest in the arts. This upsurge affected all intellectuals in the city. Harold and some of his friends were budding intellectuals. They made fun of the sentimental songs and movies, even when they enjoyed them. Harold had been writing poetry since he was twelve years old. He visited the

悬崖因此是一个重要的象征。这首歌的作者，美国人尼克·伯顿在歌词中犯了个错误，写了"多佛的白色峭壁有蓝鸟"。伯顿不知蓝鸟是美国特有的鸟类。在美国歌曲和故事中，蓝鸟象征着幸福。然而，英国人并不介意这一白璧微瑕，甚至乐于接受，他们将蓝鸟当做一种承诺，一种美好时光会再来的象征。英国作曲家休·查利写了另一首流行歌曲《我们会再见》，许多家庭想念在前线打仗的丈夫、儿子和父亲，《我们会再见》表达了人们与亲人重逢的希望。

哈罗德并不沉醉于这些流行歌所表达的情感。作为一名犹太青年，他并不排斥犹太文化传统，这种传统十分注重思辨能力、抽象思维和文化艺术。在战争期间的伦敦，艺术有抬头之势，影响了伦敦的所有知识分子。哈罗德和他的一些朋友是新露头角的知识分子。他们嘲弄煽情的歌曲和电影，即便自己喜欢这些作品也照嘲弄不误。哈罗德12岁开始写诗。他常去

Hackney Public Library often. He could read difficult literature, such as that of poets Arthur Rimbaud[1] and Ezra Pound[2], as well as the prose of James Joyce.

At fourteen years of age, Harold joined a film club. He saw American films, Russian films, and European films, as well as British ones. One of his favorite films was *Un Chien Andalou*[3], or, in English, *Andalusian Dog*. This art film was made in 1929 by the Spanish director, Luis Buñel[4]. It features Salvador Dali[5], the famous surrealist artist, also Spanish. The movie shows striking images in a loosely connected series of events — the most famous being an eyeball sliced with a razor. The logic of the movie isn't typical of a story. It has an unreal quality that showed the young Harold a new kind of narration.

1. Arthur Rimbaud: 阿蒂尔·兰波 (1854–1891)，19世纪法国著名诗人，早期象征主义诗歌的代表人物，超现实主义诗歌的鼻祖

2. Ezra Pound: 埃兹拉·庞德 (1885–1972)，美国著名意象派诗人、文学家。庞德热衷于介绍中国古典诗歌和哲学，他改编并翻译了《华夏集》(*Cathay*, 1915)、《诗经》等

3. *Un Chien Andalou*: 《一条安达鲁狗》，由路易斯·布努艾尔和萨尔瓦多·达利联合拍摄的电影，是20世纪20年代先锋派运动中最著名的超现实主义电影。影片没有传统意义上的情节，给人松散混乱之感

4. Luis Buñel: 路易斯·布努艾尔 (1900–1983)，西班牙著名电影导演、电影剧作家、制片人，代表作有《一条安达鲁狗》、《青楼怨妇》，执导电影时擅长运用超现实主义的表现手法，与抽象派名画家达利是搭档好友

5. Salvador Dali: 萨尔瓦多·达利 (1904–1989)，西班牙超现实主义画家，作品将怪异梦境般的形象与卓越的绘画技巧相结合。代表画作为《记忆的坚持》(*The Persistence of Memory*, 1931)

哈克尼公共图书馆。他能够阅读晦涩的文学作品，诸如阿蒂尔·兰波和埃兹拉·庞德的诗，以及詹姆斯·乔伊斯的散文。

14 岁时，哈罗德加入了一个电影协会。他看美国、俄罗斯、欧洲和英国的电影。他喜爱的一部电影叫 *Un Chien Andalou*，即《一条安达鲁狗》。这是部由西班牙导演路易斯·布努艾尔于 1929 年拍摄的艺术片。片中出演者有西班牙超现实主义艺术家萨尔瓦多·达利。电影用一组松散的事件展现了突出的影像——最著名的影像是眼珠被剃须刀切开。这部电影的逻辑不是典型的故事逻辑。它具有非现实的特性，向年轻的哈罗德展示了一种新的叙事方式。

The war and all that it called into question brought out Harold's skepticism. The serious arts offered him new ways to look at life. As he rejected conventional religious belief, he also began to reject conventional methods of storytelling. New literary and movie techniques offered models of a willingness to disregard accepted ideals. These unconventional artistic explorations of new ideals were important to Harold. They influenced his personal life and, later, his literary work.

战争及其引发的问题让哈罗德产生怀疑。严肃艺术为他提供了看待生活的新方式。他不但开始排斥传统的宗教信仰，也开始排斥传统的叙事方式。新的文艺和电影技巧给他提供了一个拒绝接受现成观念的榜样。这些新的理念和艺术探索的新方式，对哈罗德至关重要，它们影响了哈罗德的个人生活和他后来的文学作品。

Chapter Five

FRIENDS AND ENEMIES

朋友和敌人

*H*arold was growing up. He was more and more interested in girls, one girl in particular[1]. He saw her go by on his street sometimes. He thought she was pretty, but he didn't know how to get her to like him. Then he got an idea. He knew lots of English girls dated American soldiers. United States soldiers had started arriving in London in 1942. By 1944, there were many of them. American soldiers were disliked by some Londoners because they could be arrogant[2], acting like they could win World War II all by themselves. However, they were good-natured and kind with children, giving them gum and candy. They also had more money to spend than British soldiers did. They could take their dates out to better restaurants and shows.

He found out the girl's telephone number, and then he called her up and pretended to be an American soldier. In a fake American accent, he told her he'd seen her around and thought she was cute. He asked her to meet him at a nearby park.

"Who is this? How did you get my phone number?" asked the girl. She didn't say that she would meet him, but she didn't hang up on[3] him either.

1. in particular: *adv.* 特别，特别是
2. arrogant: *adj.* 傲慢的，自大的
3. hang up on sb: 挂断某人的电话

哈罗德逐渐长大，对女孩子越来越感兴趣，尤其钟情于一位女孩。他有时在街边看到她走过，觉得她很美，可又不知如何让她爱上自己。后来他想到了办法。他知道许多英国女孩喜欢和美国士兵约会。美国士兵从1942年起陆续来到伦敦，到1944年，伦敦已经有了许多美国士兵。美国士兵招致许多伦敦人的反感，因为他们傲慢，好像可以独自打赢二战一样。不过，他们对孩子却和蔼亲切，给孩子们口香糖和糖果。与英国士兵相比，他们更有钱，可以带女友去更高档的餐馆，看更精彩的演出。

哈罗德找到那女孩的电话号码，然后假装美国士兵给她打电话。他装成美国口音，说在附近见过她，觉得她很可爱，约她在附近公园见面。

"你是谁？你怎么知道我电话号码的？"女孩问道。她没说是否赴约，却也没挂电话。

It was a rainy day when Harold walked out to go to the park to see if the girl would come when he'd asked her to. He stood by the park gates and waited. A few minutes later, the girl appeared.

"Harold Pinter!" she exclaimed[1] , surprised to see him where she was supposed to[2] meet the soldier. It didn't take long for her to realize that Harold was the "American soldier". She was a little angry, but also a little flattered by his trick. They became boyfriend and girlfriend for about a year. She was the first girl that Harold fell in love with.

Harold's mother thought Harold was too young to have a girlfriend. His father didn't complain about the girl. Harold sometimes felt like his father complained about everything else though. Jack complained about big things and little things. He complained about Harold's not following the Jewish religion. He complained if Harold didn't clear the dishes off the table fast enough after they ate. He complained about Harold's needing to shine his shoes or get a haircut. However much his parents yelled and fussed, Harold knew he was their darling. They adored him and wanted him to do well. They encouraged his poetry writing, and they made sure he studied.

Harold was a student at Grocer's Company

1. exclaim : *v.* 呼喊, 惊叫, 大声叫
2. be supposed to do sth : 预期做某事, 理应做某事

那是个下雨天, 哈罗德离开家, 走到公园, 看女孩是否准时出现。他站在公园门口等着。几分钟后, 女孩现身了。

"哈罗德·品特!" 她大声叫着, 很惊讶见到的是品特, 而不是美国士兵。不过, 女孩很快就知道哈罗德正是那位 "美国士兵"。她有些生气, 但也为哈罗德的把戏感到惊喜。他们相恋了一年左右。她是哈罗德的初恋。

哈罗德的母亲认为哈罗德年纪尚轻, 谈情说爱为时过早。他的父亲并不嫌弃这个女孩。可是除此之外, 哈罗德有时感觉父亲什么都抱怨, 大事抱怨, 小事也抱怨。他抱怨哈罗德没有信奉犹太教, 抱怨哈罗德没能在饭后及时把碗碟撤下桌子, 抱怨哈罗德把皮鞋擦得锃亮, 又抱怨他理的发型。不论父母如何大惊小怪、大呼小叫, 哈罗德都知道自己是父母的最爱。他们爱他, 想他好。他们也鼓励他写诗, 督促他学习。

哈罗德在格罗器公司高级中学, 又名哈克尼下区文法学校就读。这

High School, also known as Hackney Downs Grammar School. It was a good school. The teachers and students had high standards and great regard for learning. Most of the students were Jewish. At this school there was a popular teacher, an English teacher, named Joe Brearley. Brearley passed on his passion for English poetry and drama to Pinter and other pupils. He took Harold and some of his friends to see Shakespeare performances by excellent actors. He went with them for long walks from Hackney Downs School all around the neighborhood, reciting[1] passages from Shakespeare and other great English poets. Brearley was to become Pinter's lifelong friend.

Harold also formed lifelong friendships at the Hackney Boys Club he belonged to. He went to the club after school to hang out[2] with other boys. They played table-tennis there. They joked and argued as well. Harold and his closest friends enjoyed competing in the realm[3] of ideas as well as in the realm of sports.

1. recite: *v.* 背诵，朗读
2. hang out *v.* (口语)常去某处
hang out with sb: 常和某人
呆在一起
3. realm: *n.* 领域，境界

Because they were poor, they walked almost everywhere they went. They shared poverty and ideas. The boys all shared their interests. For one or two boys, classical music was their love. They got the others interested in it too. Harold shared his love of literature.

是所不错的学校，老师和学生对待学习要求都严，大家都尊重学问。学生大多是犹太人。学校有位英语老师很受欢迎，名叫乔·布里尔利。布里尔利将他对英国诗歌和戏剧的激情灌输给品特和其他学生。他带哈罗德和他的一些朋友一起看由出色演员演出的莎士比亚剧作。他和学生们一起徒步出游，从哈克尼下区文法学校走遍整个社区，一路背诵莎士比亚和其他伟大英国诗人的作品。布里尔利后来成为品特的终生好友。

哈罗德还在自己所属的哈克尼男孩俱乐部里结交了许多终生好友。他放学后去俱乐部，和其他男孩乐在一起。他们在那儿打乒乓球、开玩笑、辩论。除了体育上的竞技，哈罗德和挚友们还喜欢思想上的竞技。

因为囊中羞涩，他们几乎到什么地方都是步行。他们分享着贫穷，也分享着志趣。只要有一两个男孩对古典音乐感兴趣，就会让其他人也产生兴趣。哈罗德和大家分享他对文学的热爱。

He read difficult books and encouraged his friends to read them. Since reading *Ulysses* and upsetting his father with that scandalous[1] book, he had read the famous Russian novel, *Crime and Punishment*. He read the poetry of Welsh poet Dylan Thomas[2]. He read French poet Arthur Rimbaud's *The Drunken Boat* and *A Season in Hell*. One of the books he read and enjoyed most was John Steinbeck[3]'s *Of Mice and Men*. Steinbeck's book meant a lot to Harold. The book is about a friendship between two men who work on a ranch[4] in California. Lennie, one of the men, is mentally retarded[5]. Lennie doesn't understand much about what is going on around him. George, the other man is normal in intelligence and protects Lennie from harm as much as he can. They have been friends for years. One day Lennie accidentally kills a woman. George knows Lennie didn't mean to hurt her. He also knows Lennie will be captured, put in jail, and hanged for her death. George makes a heart-breaking decision. He shoots Lennie to spare him the horror of capture, jail, and

1. scandalous: *adj.* 丢脸的，令人震惊的，令人愤慨的
2. Dylan Thomas: 迪伦·托马斯(1914–1953)是威尔士英语诗人。其诗歌受到现代主义诗歌和浪漫主义传统的双重影响，技巧圆熟，关注读者的情感诉求，具有强烈的抒情性，被认为是自奥登之后最重要的诗人
3. John Steinbeck: 约翰·斯坦贝克(1902–1968)是美国作家，小说《愤怒的葡萄》(*The Grapes of Wrath*, 1939)获1940年普利策奖。斯坦贝克写过16部小说，6部非小说和其他短篇小说集，并获1962年诺贝尔文学奖
4. ranch: *n.* 大农场，牧场
5. retard: *v.* 延迟，阻挡，阻碍

他读晦涩的书，也鼓励朋友读这些书。自从阅读《尤利西斯》以来——读这本引起争议的书让他父亲很失望——他又读了俄国名著《罪与罚》。他读威尔士诗人迪伦·托马斯的诗，法国诗人阿蒂尔·兰波的《醉舟》和《地狱的一季》。他最喜欢的书是约翰·斯坦贝克的《鼠与人》。斯坦贝克的书对哈罗德意义重大。这本书讲述两个加州农场的男工之间的友情。两人之一的莱尼是智障，不太清楚发生在其周围的事。另外一人乔治则是正常人，他尽力保护莱尼免受伤害。他们是多年的好友。有一天莱尼误杀了个女人。乔治知道莱尼本不想伤害她。他知道莱尼全被捕、坐牢，并被绞死，于是做了个让人伤心的决定：将莱尼枪杀，以免莱尼遭受被捕、坐牢、被绞死的恐惧。乔治知道没有他在身边，莱尼

hanging. He knows that Lennie will be scared and confused without George beside him. Because he loves Lennie and doesn't want him to suffer, he shoots Lennie just as the other ranch hands come to get him.

Loyalty and fairness are major issues in this novel. It made a deep impression on Harold. Later in life, Harold would discover author Samuel Beckett, whose most famous play "Waiting for Godot", has been compared to *Of Mice and Men*. Beckett would be the greatest literary influence on Harold Pinter's work.

Being interested in fairness, Harold was interested in politics. He shared with his friends his happiness about the Labour Party[1] victory in the British election of 1945. As a working-class youngster, he felt sure his friends and family would benefit from having that party in power. The Labor Party would understand the problems of the poor he felt sure.

Both poverty and their Jewish background joined most of the boys in Harold's group of friends. These two circumstances, which set them apart[2] from many other Londoners, strengthened their loyalty to each other. They all opposed fascism.

1. Labour Party: 英国工党，成立于1900年2月27日，是英国的主要政党之一。工党纲领的传统理论基础是费边社会主义。二战后推行温和的改革政策，推行国有化，主张建立福利型国家

2. set apart: v. 使分离，使分开

　　会感到恐惧和困惑。他爱莱尼，不想他担惊受怕，故而在农场其他人来抓莱尼之前，枪杀了莱尼。

　　忠诚和公平是这部小说的主题，它对哈罗德影响深刻。后来，哈罗德发现了塞缪尔·贝克特的名剧《等待戈多》。该剧被拿来和《鼠与人》比较。贝克特后来成为对哈罗德作品影响最大的作家。

　　出于对公平的兴趣，哈罗德对政治感兴趣起来。工党在1945年英国大选中获胜，他和朋友们分享了这一喜悦。作为一个工薪阶层的年轻人，他确信亲朋好友会受益于工党的执政。他相信工党会理解穷人所面临的难题。

　　哈罗德的朋友大都是贫穷和有犹太背景的男孩。这两种情况使他们和许多伦敦人分隔开来，也增进了彼此之间的忠诚。他们都反对法西斯主义。很奇怪，尽管反法西斯主义的战争已获得胜利，伦敦报摊仍在

Surprisingly, though the war against fascism had been won, fascist newspapers and magazines still sold on the newsstands[1] in London. Even ordinary people sometimes showed a hatred of Jews. Knowing that millions of Jews were killed by the Nazis in World War II, Harold and his friends knew where ordinary people's hatred could lead.

It's no wonder that Harold hated injustice. He was outspoken[2] too. If he thought something was unfair, he said so. If he was punished at school, he would accept the punishment if he felt it was fair. If he thought he'd been unfairly treated, he went to the headmaster to complain. He had some of his father's temper. He would allow no one to bully[3] him.

The East End was a rough neighborhood. There were plenty of bullies around. One afternoon, as Harold and four of his friends walked along the sidewalk, they heard a shout from a nearby group of boys. One of the boys pointed at Harold's friend Jimmy and called out "Commie[4]".

Jimmy held his book up and asked, "Why because I can read?"

Jimmy, Harold, Mick, and their two other friends laughed at Jimmy's clever insult. They walked on. The gang of thugs[5] followed them.

1. newsstand: *n.* 报摊, 杂志摊
2. outspoken: *adj.* 坦率直言的, 直言不讳的
3. bully: *v.* 欺负, 欺凌(弱小)
4. Commie: *n.* 对共产党员的戏称
5. thug: *n.* 暴徒, 凶手

出售法西斯报刊。连普通人有时也会表现出对犹太人的憎恨。成千上万的犹太人在二战中被纳粹杀害, 哈罗德和朋友们知道普通人的仇恨可能会引发多大的灾难。

所以, 难怪哈罗德会憎恨不公平。他也直言不讳。遇见不公, 他会毫不隐晦地说出来。如果他在学校被罚, 觉得公平, 他就会坦然接受。假使他觉得受到不公平的待遇, 他会直接去向校长申诉。他的脾气有些像他父亲, 容不得别人欺负。

伦敦东区是个粗野的社区, 这里有很多恶霸。一天下午, 哈罗德正和四个朋友在街边走着, 听到附近一群男孩喊他们。其中一个男孩指着哈罗德的朋友吉米, 叫他"共匪"。

吉米举起书反问道, "难道就因为我能读书吗?"

吉米、哈罗德和米克, 还有其他两位朋友为吉米机智的回答笑了起

Harold and Mick trailed behind the other three boys by several yards. The friends in front had already turned a corner when an enormous onion hit the wall of the bank Harold and Mick were walking past. One of the gang had thrown it. Mick grabbed Harold to hurry him. Harold wouldn't hurry. He turned to face the thugs. Mick ran ahead to get the other friends. When they got back around the corner, Harold was surrounded by six rough-looking boys. Some of the boys held bike chains in their hands. These chains could be used as weapons. They could be slung, like a whip, against someone's face. They could be wrapped around the fist, like "brass knuckles[1]", to make a punch hurt more. A couple of the gang members held the jagged tops of milk bottles broken off at the neck. Jimmy rushed forward and forced his way through the ring of boys. He stood next to Harold. Together the two faced the gang.

Luckily, just at that time, a trolleybus[2] slowed down to get around the corner. Mick motioned to the driver to stop. The gang surrounding Harold and Jimmy hid their weapons behind their backs. When the bus driver stopped the bus, Harold and his friends got onto the trolley. The gang of boys on

1. brass knuckles: *n.* 指节铜环（套于指节上作武器用的指节铜套）
2. trolleybus: *n.* 无轨电车

来。他们继续走着，这帮恶棍就跟在后头。哈罗德和米克走在其他三人之后，相距几码。前面的朋友转过街角时，一个大洋葱头击中哈罗德和米克正走过的银行的墙上。那是其中一个恶棍扔的。米克抓住哈罗德催他快点走。哈罗德并不慌张，他转过身，面对这群恶棍。米克跑去叫其他朋友。他们回来时，哈罗德已被六个粗野的男孩围住。有些男孩手中拿着自行车链子——他们拿它当武器，可以像鞭子一样把人打得满脸开花，也可以缠在拳头上，当做"指节铜套"，这样拳头打人更疼。有几个恶棍则拿着锯齿状的碎牛奶瓶瓶口。吉米跑上前去，挤过这群男孩，站在哈罗德身边，两人一起面对这帮人。

说来也巧，就在此时，一辆无轨电车放慢速度转过街角。米克示意司机停车。包围哈罗德和吉米的这帮人把武器藏在身后。司机停住车，

the street yelled at them as the bus pulled away. The friends on the bus laughed. They congratulated each other on their good fortune. They would've fought if they had to, but they were smart enough to get on the bus and avoid serious trouble.

哈罗德和朋友们上了电车。电车开走时，那帮男孩向他们喊叫。车上，几个朋友笑了起来。他们庆祝好运气。要是迫不得已，他们会打起来，但他们很机灵地上了电车，避免了麻烦。

Chapter Six

BEGINNINGS AND ENDINGS

开始和结束

*B*efore high school was over, Harold had found a new purpose in life. It didn't replace his old pleasures, like sports, but it would lead him into playwriting and fame. In high school, as in later life, Harold wanted to succeed, on his own terms. In high school, he succeeded academically[1] and in sports. Harold played center-forward in soccer. In his later life, he said that he wasn't above cheating to gain a point. In one high school game that was played between teams at his school, he pretended to be hurt.

"Oh, oh," he groaned[2], falling onto the ground as though he were in pain. The game was stopped, and Harold quickly got up and ran to the goal. This kind of trickery[3] came from his drive to succeed. Harold played to win. Winning was important to Pinter. It was so important that he may have projected his own feelings onto a classmate — he accused his classmate of never forgiving Pinter for beating him in a race. Though Pinter certainly never forgot beating his classmate, it's not clear how he could be sure his classmate never forgave him for it. He himself wouldn't forget such a loss if he'd suffered it.

It's understandable that Harold didn't forget the victory. He competed against the best runner in

1. academically: *adv.* 学术上，学理上
2. groan: *v.* 呻吟，呻吟着
3. trickery: *n.* 欺骗

高中毕业前，哈罗德找到了新的人生目标。虽然这并未取代体育之类的旧爱好，但这个新目标，却让他走上了戏剧创作之路，并给他带来了声誉。从高中时起，哈罗德就想按照自己的意愿走上成功之路。高中阶段，他在学习和体育上都很成功。哈罗德是足球中锋。后来他回忆说，为了得分他不惜欺骗。高中时，在一场比赛中，他曾假装受伤。

"哎哟，哎哟，"他呻吟着，那样子好像痛苦不堪。比赛暂停时，哈罗德马上起身跑向球门。要这样的把戏是因他求胜心切。哈罗德参加比赛就是为了赢。得胜对他很重要，他甚至把这种心态推己及人，投射到他的一个同学身上了：这位同学曾与他比赛短跑，输了，品特说那同学一直耿耿于怀，不肯原谅自己。品特当然忘不了这次胜利，可是不知他为何这么肯定同学不肯原谅他。不过，他自己要是输了，绝对会受不了的。

得胜之后，哈罗德沾沾自喜。这可以理解：他和学校最优秀的短跑

school. This runner was well trained. He was an excellent stylist. Still, Harold beat him. Harold won through "brute force", by pushing himself fiercely to the finish line. In that race, he broke the school record for sprinting. This success meant a great deal to him. Another high school success meant even more to him.

In high school, Harold got a chance to act on stage. Joe Brearley, his favorite teacher, gave Harold the role of Macbeth[1] in the school's production of Shakespeare's tragedy of the same name. Harold was pleased to take the leading role in the play. This role of an ambitious, brooding[2] man, capable of murder, is one of the best known of all Shakespeare's characters. Harold often described himself as morose[3], and Shakespeare's Macbeth could certainly be described as morose, too. Harold's voice had changed by the time he took on this role. He no longer had the voice of a boy. He had a deep voice, full of power. This voice lent itself well to the role of Macbeth. Harold's appearance was also striking. He was tall and handsome, with dark hair and dark eyes.

1. Macbeth: 麦克白，是莎士比亚悲剧《麦克白》中的人物。麦克白是中世纪苏格兰的一名骁将，三个女巫预言他将成为国王，麦克白夫人野心勃勃，鼓动他弑君。当麦克白登上王位后，他发现自己并不幸福，鲜血与罪恶感时刻在折磨着这位苏格兰新王，在新的内战中，麦克白被杀

2. brooding: *adj.* 忧郁的，沉思的

3. morose: *adj.* 郁闷的，乖僻的

选手竞赛。这位短跑选手受过良好的训练，也颇有风度，但哈罗德还是打败了他。哈罗德以"蛮力"获胜。他全力追赶，直到终点线。那场比赛中，哈罗德打破了校短跑纪录。这对他来说意义重大。而高中时的另一次成功对他来说意义更加重大。

高中期间，哈罗德有机会登台表演。哈罗德最喜爱的老师乔·布里尔利，让他在学校编排的莎士比亚悲剧《麦克白》中扮演麦克白。哈罗德很高兴能在剧中扮演主角。麦克白这个角色富有野心，精于算计，为了达到目的，甚至不惜谋杀。他是莎士比亚作品中最广为人知的人物之一。哈罗德常形容自己性格乖僻，和莎士比亚笔下的麦克白如出一辙。在搭演这个角色前，哈罗德已经过了变声期。童声没有了，他的嗓音变得浑厚有力，与麦克白这一角色正好相配。哈罗德的外表同样令人印象

Given[1] Harold's manly voice, his personality, his appearance, and his intelligence, it's easy to see why Brearley chose him for the part.

Brearley set the play in modern times and had Pinter wear the khaki[2] uniform of a modern soldier. When Harold wore this uniform to and from school, some people thought he was a real soldier. Harold enjoyed the attention he got on the bus. He enjoyed being on stage even more. Adding to his pleasure, a newspaper drama critic gave his performance as Macbeth a good review. The critic called Harold Pinter's acting "eloquent". He said that seventeen-year-old Harold Pinter played the role as well as some professional actors. Later, after a great many successes, Pinter met this critic. He told him that he treasured that review. He said it meant more to him than any other review he'd ever gotten.

Brearley had boys play all the parts, as in theaters in Shakespeare's time. Ron Percival, one of Harold's best friends, played Lady Macbeth[3]. Ron's blonde good looks made him well-suited to the part. Though Harold liked girls, he could easily see how

1. given: 英语中用 given 做句子开头，常表示"考虑到…，有鉴于…"的意思
2. khaki: *n.* 卡其布
3. Lady Macbeth: 麦克白夫人。《麦克白》中麦克白的夫人，鼓动丈夫弑君，从而使自己成为苏格兰皇后，最后因罪恶而受到折磨

深剖：他高大英俊，黑头发黑眼睛。鉴于哈罗德富有男子气的嗓音、个性、外表以及才智，不难看出布里尔利为何会选他来扮演麦克白了。

　　布里尔利将此剧融入现代背景，让哈罗德穿上卡其布军装。哈罗德穿着军装走在上学放学路上，居然有人把他当成真的军人。哈罗德喜欢在公交车上受人关注。他更喜欢登台表演。让他更为高兴的是，一位报纸戏剧评论家对他所饰演的麦克白一角给予很高的评价，称赞哈罗德·品特的表演"雄辩有力"，还说 17 岁的哈罗德·品特的表演不逊于一些专业演员。哈罗德功成名就之后，见到了这位评论家，告诉他说自己很珍视他当时的评价，还说这个评价比后来得到的任何评价都更有意义。

　　布里尔利效仿莎士比亚时代剧院的做法，让男孩扮演所有角色。哈罗德的好友罗恩·珀西瓦尔反串麦克白夫人。罗恩皮肤白皙，相貌英俊，很配这个角色。哈罗德喜欢女孩子，但他不难看出罗恩为何能吸引其他

boys could be attracted to Ron. He felt some of that attraction. This ability to feel even forbidden feelings is important to any artist. Few men who aren't gay would admit to understanding attraction toward another man. Harold was confident enough in his manhood to say what he felt, however fleetingly, about his good friend's appeal. Another reason Harold had the courage to say what he believed is that he had lived through the terror of the blitz. He had faced death and survived. Facing other people's mere opinions held little threat for him. He and other people who survived the German air raids had a different sense of proportion than people who had lived in safety most of their lives.

Later, in another of Brearley's school productions, Harold played the part of Romeo in "Romeo and Juliet". He got a good review, but didn't get attention from a major critic as he had for his Macbeth. His imposing personality and deep voice didn't lend itself as well to the youthful sensitivity audiences expect from Romeo. In a way, Harold's presence was "heavy[1]". In his acting career, he was often chosen for the part of a villain. It would've been difficult for audiences to see him as the love-smitten[2] hero of "Romeo and Juliet".

1. heavy: *adj.* 指（人、书、风格等）严肃而沉闷的，单调乏味的
2. love-smitten: *adj.* 一见钟情的

男孩，连他自己都感到有些受吸引。感知包括禁忌情感在内的各样情感的能力，对所有艺术家都至关重要。很少有非男同性恋者承认受到其他男人吸引。哈罗德对自己的男子气概十分自信，因而敢于承认自己受到好友的吸引——哪怕只是一瞬间的感受。哈罗德经历过闪电战的恐惧，曾面对死亡并幸免于难，别人的看法对他军有威胁，所以他有什么说什么，百无禁忌。同一辈子大部分时间生活在安全中的人相比，他和那些经历过德军空袭的人一样，有着不同的分寸感。

后来，在布里尔利执导的另一部学校剧中，哈罗德扮演了《罗密欧与朱丽叶》中的罗密欧。演出获得了好评，但没有像他饰演麦克白那样，受到主要评论家的关注。他个性威严，嗓音深沉，和观众期待的年轻而敏感的罗密欧形象相距甚远。从某种程度上看，哈罗德的演绎太过"厚重"。在他的演出生涯中，他常演反角。观众很难把他和《罗密欧与朱丽叶》中一见钟情的男主角联系到一起。

Acting would be part of Pinter's life from that time on. He loved the words and rhythms of spoken language. He liked the challenge of mastering a difficult role. He enjoyed being able to move an audience to laughter, tears, or to a new insight. Joe Brearley had given him a calling. Years later, Pinter would write a poem about this fine teacher, who died in 1977. In the poem, he tells his teacher how well he remembers their long walks together. He describes Brearley as "tall in the moonlight". In the poem, he says time has passed, and they are separated. But, he says, they're also still together and always will be.

> You're gone. I'm at your side,
> Walking with you from Clapton Pond to Finsbury Park,
> And on, and on.

This poem to his teacher was written after Pinter was well-known as a playwright. Much as he liked acting and writing plays, he would continue to write poetry. Much of his urge to write poems came from his sharp awareness of the closeness of death. The sense of "unease", as he called it, was with him during the blitz as was a joy in being alive. These feelings showed in his poetry and, later, in his plays.

从此以后，表演就成为哈罗德生活的一部分。他喜欢口语的文字和节奏。他喜欢接受挑战去驾驭难以饰演的角色。他喜欢让观众大笑、流泪，或是让他们深思。乔·布里尔利帮他找到了一个终身追求。多年后，品特为这位 1977 年逝世的优秀老师写了一首诗。诗中说他还记得他们一起散步的日子。他描述布里尔利"在月光中显得越发高大"。在诗中，他说时光飞逝，他们早已分别，但仍在一起，并将永远在一起。

> 你走了。我在你身边，
> 和你一起从克拉普顿湖走到芬斯伯里公园，
> 一直走下去，一直走下去。

哈罗德是在成为著名剧作家之后，才写了这首致老师的诗。他热爱表演和编剧，但也一直坚持写诗。他写诗的想法大都来自对死亡临近的清晰认识。这种感觉他称为"不安"，和"生的喜悦"一样，这感觉在伦敦战期间一直伴随着他。这种感觉先是出现在他的诗歌中，后来又出现在他的剧作中。

In high school, he wrote many poems. Less often, he wrote prose, such as essays for the school magazine. One of the articles he wrote for his fellow students was about *Ulysses*, the novel his father so disapproved. He confidently spoke of this book as the most important novel of the twentieth century.

Though he loved books and ideas, Harold wasn't meant to be a scholar. Partly, he was too impatient. He gave some thought to trying to get into Oxford or Cambridge, but he hadn't learned Latin. He took a short course, but saw right away that he didn't want to spend the time it would take to learn it. Instead, when he graduated from Hackney Grammar School in 1948, he enrolled in the Royal Academy of Dramatic Art[1]. He got a grant to attend.

Expecting to find himself in a school that suited him, Harold was surprised to find that he hated RADA. A few years later it would be one of the most exciting places in London for young people to study acting, but when Harold entered it was still very conventional.

The year he was supposed to be learning acting there was one of his unhappiest times. None of his

> 1. the Royal Academy of Dramatic Art: 皇家戏剧学院，位于伦敦市布卢姆斯伯里，是世界上最著名的戏剧学校之一，也是英国历史最悠久的戏剧学校

哈罗德高中期间写了很多诗。他也偶尔写写散文，比如为校刊写些随笔。在一篇文章中，他向同学介绍了他父亲反对的那本《尤利西斯》。他自信地将这本书称为20世纪最重要的小说。

哈罗德喜欢读书，热爱思考，但并不想成为学者。部分原因是他不够耐心。他曾想过到牛津大学或剑桥大学读书，但又没学过拉丁文。后来进了门短期课程，很快又发现自己不想花时间学拉丁文。1948年，他从哈克尼文法学校毕业后，考入了皇家戏剧学院，并拿到了一项奖学金。

哈罗德本以为这所学校很适合自己，结果却发现他讨厌皇家戏剧学院。数年后，该学院将成为伦敦最令人向往的一个地方，年轻人在那儿学习表演，可是哈罗德入学那会儿，学院仍非常传统。

哈罗德在校学习表演的那一年是他最不开心的一段时光。他的朋友

friends went to school there. He detested the students and teachers at RADA. He thought they were self-centered. He found them out of touch with the working-class views that he held.

The dislike was mutual. Many students and teachers didn't like Harold. They found him moody and rude.

After a while, Harold began to play hookey[1] from RADA. He left his home in the morning pretending to be going to acting school. Instead, he went to the Hackney Library to read until time for his friends to get out of school. Sometimes he walked around or watched a cricket game. Finally, he faked a nervous breakdown[2] and quit attending RADA at all.

Another problem came up during this unhappy year. Harold was drafted for National Service in October 1948. Instead of agreeing to enter the army, he sent back his draft papers. He said he was a conscientious objector[3]. As with any young man who refused military service, he had to appear before a military tribunal[4]. The tribunal would rule on whether he would be allowed to stay out of the army. His parents were upset at Harold's refusal to

1. hookey: *n.* (俚语) 逃学
2. nervous breakdown: *n.* (医学) 精神失常
3. conscientious objector: *n.* 拒绝服兵役的人
4. military tribunal: *n.* 军事法庭

都不在这所学校。他讨厌皇家戏剧学院的老师和同学，认为他们太过以自我为中心。他们与他所持的劳动阶层见解格格不入。

这种厌恶是相互的。许多老师和学生也不喜欢哈罗德。他们认为他喜怒无常，粗鲁无礼。

过了段时间，哈罗德开始从皇家戏剧学院逃学。他早晨离开家，装作去学校，结果却去哈克尼图书馆读书，一直读到朋友放学的时候。有时他会到处转转或是去看板球比赛。最后，他假装精神崩溃，彻底从皇家戏剧学院辍学。

在这不愉快的一年里，他遇到了另一个问题。1948 年 10 月，哈罗德被政府征兵服役。哈罗德不愿当兵，将征兵材料寄了回去，说自己拒绝服役。同其他拒绝服役的年轻人一样，他要面对军事法庭的审判。军事法庭决定他能否免于服役。哈罗德的父母为他拒绝服役感到失望。除残

go into the army. All young men were supposed to go unless a disability or religious reasons kept them from going. This was the first serious disagreement between Harold and his parents. Up to this point, the family had been able to work out its problems without hard feelings. This was different. Jack, Frances, and Harold were all miserable. Harold's parents asked Joe Brearley to talk to Harold. They hoped Harold's favorite teacher would persuade him to go for his military service. Brearley refused to help them. He said Harold had a right to refuse and was willing to take the punishment.

At Harold's first military tribunal, in 1949, he was asked why he refused to do his service for his country. He replied that millions of people had died in World War II. He didn't want to be part of another war if one started. He wanted nothing to do with fighting a war. The tribunal didn't accept his reasons. He was allowed to appeal[1] its decision, however. In his appeal he could bring someone to vouch for[2] him. Most young men brought a teacher or religious figure, such as a pastor. Harold brought Morris Wernick, one of his young friends. Morris told the tribunal that Harold always did what he said he would do.

"If he says he's not going to serve, then you can be sure he's serious about it," said Morris.

> 1. appeal: v. 上诉
> 2. vouch for: v. 担保，保证

疾或宗教原因之外，年轻人都应当服役。这是哈罗德和父母首次出现严重分歧。此前，品特一家都能心平气和地解决问题，不伤感情。但这次却不同。杰克、弗朗西斯和哈罗德都感到伤心。哈罗德的父母请乔·布里尔利来开导哈罗德。他们希望哈罗德最喜爱的老师能劝他去服兵役。布里尔利不愿帮他们这个忙，反说哈罗德有权拒绝服役，再说他也愿意接受惩罚。

1949年，哈罗德第一次上军事法庭，法庭问他为何拒绝为国家服役，他回答说二战中千百万人死去，如果有人再次发动战争，那他不想参与，他不想打仗。军事法庭没有接受他的理由。不过，他获准上诉。上诉时，他可以请人为自己担保。大多数年轻人请老师或者牧师等神职人员出庭。哈罗德请他的年轻好友莫里斯·韦尼克出庭。莫里斯告诉军事法庭，哈罗德向来说到做到。

"如果他说不愿服役，那一定是很较真的，"莫里斯说。

This statement didn't explain the reasons for Harold's refusal, so it was of no help. Harold's appeal was dismissed[1].

Harold expected to be sent to prison. Morris was getting ready to go to the army. When they got out of the courtroom, they took off on a trip without telling anyone where they were going. They spent a week hitch-hiking around Cornwall. It was summer, and they enjoyed themselves roaming around Mevagissey, near where Harold had stayed during his evacuation to Caerhays Castle.

Harold received another set of call up papers. He refused to take the medical exam required in the papers so they could make sure he was fit for service to the army. He was arrested and taken to police court[2]. Then he was called to face a civil magistrate[3]. The magistrate fined him fifty pounds. His father paid this large sum of money. This wasn't the end of his problems, however. He was called to account again in another trial and fined again. This time the fine[4] was seventy-five pounds. Again Jack Pinter paid his son's fine. Two trials[5] were the most that could be held in such cases. The matter was dropped, and Harold's father didn't have to pay any more fines. Jack's love

1. dismiss: *v.* 驳回
2. police court: *n.* 治安法庭
3. magistrate: *n.* 法官，行政长官
4. fine: *n.* 罚款，罚金
5. trial: *n.* 审判；试验

该陈述未能说明哈罗德缘何拒绝服役，故而无济于事。哈罗德的上诉被驳回。

哈罗德原本以为会下监狱。莫里森已经准备去参军。他们离开法庭后就出走了，没人知道他们去了哪里。他们在康沃尔附近转了一个星期，一路搭便车。那时候还是夏天，他们高兴地逗留于梅瓦吉西附近。梅瓦吉西离哈罗德过去疏散中所住的卡尔海斯城堡不远。

哈罗德再一次收到征兵令。征兵令文件要求他去体检，以确定他是否符合服役条件，但他没去参加体检，于是再次被捕，被送至治安法庭。随后他被传唤去见民事法官。法官判罚他50英镑。哈罗德的父亲付了这一大笔钱。然而，问题还没结束。他后来又遭传唤，再次被审，再次受罚。这一次罚金为75英镑。杰克·品特又一次为儿子付了罚款。这种案件最多可以审两次。于是案件就此了结，哈罗德的父亲不用再付罚款了。

for his son shows in his paying these heavy fines to keep his son out of jail. He paid these fines even though he disagreed with his son's decision. He had worked hard for what little money he had. It must have been painful to lose these sums to what seemed to him wrong-headed stubbornness.

Harold Pinter's personality was formed by that time. He was strong-willed and unafraid of offending people — sometimes he enjoyed offending people. He was fiercely competitive. An intense person, he entered into things he cared about with a will.

At nineteen years of age, Harold Pinter had won an important battle with the establishment. But he had been alone in an important sense. No one of his family or close friends shared his feelings about the military service. For the first time in a long time, he felt lonely.

杰克对儿子的爱就表现在付这些高额罚金来保释儿子上。他不赞同哈罗德的决定，但还是付了罚款。杰克的工作很辛苦，钱赚得也不多。因儿子执拗而付出这么大的代价，对他来说想必是件痛苦的事。

哈罗德·品特的个性到那时已经形成。他意志坚定，不惧怕得罪人——有时他还喜欢得罪人。他极富竞争性，充满激情，遇到喜欢的事情，他会不折不挠地去做。

19岁时，哈罗德·品特就在同社会制度的斗争中获得了重大胜利。但从某种意义上来说，他一直孤身应战。亲朋好友都不赞同他拒绝服兵役。他头一次感到了孤独。

Chapter Seven

IRELAND AND BACK

往返爱尔兰

*I*n 1950, Harold still lived at home. He wasn't in college, but he was reading and writing as much as if he had been in school. Two of his poems were published in the August 1950 issue of *Poetry London*. This recognition[1] of the value of his poems pleased him and his parents. *Poetry London* was the most respected poetry magazine in London at that time.

One poem "New Year in the Midlands", was a vivid, energetic poem based on a visit to a pub during his short time with the Chesterfield repertory theater[2]. The other poem, "Chandelier and Shadows," was a more serious poem. Harold's two poems appeared under his pen name, Harold Pinta. Harold chose the pen name "Pinta" because he thought his family name was originally "da Pinta", and that he was of Portuguese ancestry[3]. He claimed this ancestry was the source of his fiery temper. He found out later that the aunt who'd told him he had Portuguese ancestors was wrong. He had to give other explanations for his fiery temper.

Harold didn't want to stay at home. He was a grown man, eager to get out into the world and begin his career. He stayed busy at home, however,

1. recognition: *n.* 承认，认可
2. repertory theater: *n.* 轮演剧院，有固定剧团定期换剧目的剧场，拥有大量常备剧目的戏院
3. ancestry: *n.* 祖先，血统

1950 年，哈罗德仍在家住。他没去大学，但和在学校一样，仍旧读书写作。他的两首诗刊登在 1950 年 8 月的《伦敦诗歌》上。《伦敦诗歌》是当时伦敦最受尊敬的诗歌杂志。诗歌的价值能获得认可，他和父母都感到高兴。

《在内陆的新年》是首活泼有力的诗，讲述他在切斯特菲尔德轮演剧院短期演出期间一次逛酒馆的经历。另一首诗《吊灯和阴影》则更为严肃。两首诗发表时用的都是笔名哈罗德·平塔。用"平塔"这个笔名，是因为他猜测自己的姓氏原本是 da Pinta。他认为自己有葡萄牙血统，并声称他的火暴脾气就是这血统造成的。一个姑妈告诉他当时说他祖籍葡萄牙，后来他发现姑妈的说法不对，于是又给自己的暴躁另寻借口了。

哈罗德不想呆在家里。他已长大成人，渴望去闯荡世界，去开创一番事业。不过，他在家也没闲着，一直坚持写散文作品和诗歌。他开始

writing prose as well as poetry. He started his autobiography, *The Queen of all the Fairies*, named after a bawdy[1] song he and his friends sang when they were boys.

He stayed busy writing letters, too. He wrote letter after letter to different repertory theaters and radio stations to try to find acting jobs. He found a few small parts in theater and on the radio, but these jobs were all short-lived.

He went back to drama school for awhile. He attended the Central School of Speech and Drama. There he was more successful than he had been at the Royal Academy of Dramatic Art. The teachers and students could see his talent. With his deep voice and his imposing height, he seemed to have a promising future. This second experience in drama school was much more rewarding than his earlier one. Instead of playing hookey, as he had at the first acting school, he worked hard to learn the art of acting.

At the Central School of Speech and Drama, Harold met a young woman, Dilys Hamlett. Dilys was a drama student there, too. They talked, met for coffee, and soon became lovers. Their affair didn't last long, however. Dilys was independent, and Harold was possessive[2]. He wanted the two of them

1. bawdy: *adj.* 好色的，下流的
2. possessive: *adj.* 占有的，占有欲的

写自传《众仙女之后》，书名取自他和朋友们小时候唱的一首黄色歌曲。

他也在不断写信，给不同的轮演剧院和广播电台一封接一封地写，想找份演戏的差事。一些剧院和电台给了他几个小角色，可是为期都不长。

不久，他又去读戏校了，上的是中央戏剧演讲学校。在这所学校，他比在皇家戏剧学院时更成功些。老师和同学都注意到了他的才华。他嗓音深沉，身材高大，看上去前途光明。这回上戏校，他的收获比上回大。他不再逃学，而是努力学习表演艺术。

在中央戏剧演讲学校，哈罗德遇到了一个年轻女子迪莉斯·哈姆雷特。迪莉斯也是戏剧学校的学生。他们一起交谈，一同喝咖啡，很快就成了恋人。不过他们的恋情并不长久。迪莉斯很独立，哈罗德则占有欲旺盛。哈罗德希望两人合租一间公寓，但迪莉斯不想与他同居。他们磕

to rent an apartment together, but she didn't want to move in with him. They had a troubled affair for several months, but she began seeing another man. She and Harold broke up, and she married her new sweetheart. Harold was hurt. He still cared about her. Then his luck changed, and his mind turned to other things.

At last his letter-writing had paid off[1]. In July 1951, he got an acting job with a touring company in Ireland. The touring company belonged to Anew MacMaster. MacMaster was a well-known Shakespearean actor. Working for him would be both interesting and difficult. As part of MacMaster's company, Harold rehearsed six plays in two weeks in Dublin. Harold was assigned several parts during the rehearsal[2] period. Among these parts were three small parts in Shakespeare's *Othello*. Like the other actors, Harold had to memorize his lines quickly. He had only a short time to get ready for their first performance.

After the two weeks' rehearsal period, the company toured Irish towns, such as Waterford and Sligo. In these towns, the company actors performed the six plays they'd rehearsed. During performances in

1. pay off: *v.* 获得回报，报偿
2. rehearsal: *n.* 排练，彩排

磕磕碰碰的恋爱持续了几个月后，迪莉斯开始和别的男人约会。她和哈罗德分手后便和新男友结了婚。哈罗德很受打击。他仍在乎迪莉斯。但他后来运气好转，心思也转向了别的事情。

他写的那些信终于得到了回报。1951年7月，他得到了爱尔兰一家巡回演出剧团的演员职位。该巡回演出剧团属安纽·麦克马斯特所有。麦克马斯特是著名的莎士比亚戏剧演员，为他工作既有趣，又有挑战性。品特在两个星期之内，在都柏林和该剧团一起彩排了六个剧本。彩排期间，剧团安排哈罗德扮演不同角色，其中包括莎士比亚《奥赛罗》中的三个小角色。同其他演员一样，哈罗德必须很快记住台词。首演之前，他只有很短的时间准备。

经过两周彩排，剧团开始在爱尔兰小镇巡回演出，这些小镇包括沃特福德和斯莱戈。在这些小镇，剧团演员们表演排练的六部戏剧。在小镇巡演期间，哈罗德学到了更多演技。他留心观察麦克马斯特如何吸引

these small towns, Harold learned more about acting. He watched MacMaster win the attention of even the most rowdy[1] audiences. Harold improved in his acting. MacMaster soon trusted him with larger parts. Before this six-month tour was over, MacMaster had assigned Harold a leading part. The director gave him the role of one of Shakespeare's greatest villains[2], Iago, in *Othello*[3]

During Harold's time with the company, he didn't just act in *Othello*. He performed in two Agatha Christie[4] mysteries and in three plays by Oscar Wilde[5]. Harold would stay with MacMaster's company for two years. During that time, he learned a great deal from that gifted Shakespearean actor-director.

During his tour with the company, Harold fell in love again. Pauline Flanagan, who was also in the troop, was one of the leading actors in the company. Harold and Pauline shared a love of theater and literature. They spent almost every spare moment

1. rowdy: *adj.* 粗暴的，吵闹的
2. villain: *n.* 坏人，恶棍
3. *Othello*: 《奥赛罗》是莎士比亚四大悲剧之一，讲述威尼斯国黑人将军奥赛罗与苔丝狄梦娜的爱情悲剧
4. Agatha Christie: 阿加莎·克里斯蒂（1890 – 1976）是英国女侦探小说家、剧作家，最为人熟知的作品为《东方快车谋杀案》(*Murder on the Orient Express*, 1934) 和《尼罗河上的惨案》(*Death on the Nile*, 1937)
5. Oscar Wilde: 奥斯卡·王尔德（1854 – 1900）是英国唯美主义艺术运动的倡导者，作家、诗人、戏剧家、艺术家，主要作品包括小说《道林·格雷的画像》(*The Picture of Dorian Gray*, 1891)、戏剧《温德密尔夫人的扇子》(*Lady Windermere's Fan*, 1892)、《认真的重要性》(*The Importance of Being Earnest*, 1895) 等。王尔德的戏剧充满智慧，妙语连珠

观众，包括那些最喧闹的观众。哈罗德的演技也有所提高。麦克马斯特不久就开始信任他，让他扮演更重要的角色。为期半年的巡回演出结束之前，麦克马斯特安排哈罗德演主要角色了。这位导演将莎士比亚笔下最著名的反角之一、《奥赛罗》中的伊阿古一角给了哈罗德。

哈罗德在剧团演出期间，他不仅在《奥赛罗》一剧中表演，还在两部阿加莎·克里斯蒂的悬念剧和三部奥斯卡·王尔德的剧中演出。哈罗德在麦克马斯特的剧团呆了两年。在此期间，他从这位极具天赋的莎士比亚导演兼演员身上学到很多东西。

在剧团期间，哈罗德又恋爱了。这回他恋上了剧团的一位主演保利娜·弗拉纳根。哈罗德和保利娜都喜欢戏剧和文学。演出之余，他们多

together. When they took a break from the tour, Harold took her to London to meet his parents. In London, he took her to the movies. He was still a great fan of films. They saw *Los Olvidadoes*[1], directed by Luis Buñel. Buñel, director of one of Harold's favorites, *Un Chien Andalou,* had an artistic style that Harold admired. This film director's artistic influence would become apparent in Harold's writing and acting.

Harold's mother liked Pauline, but she was concerned — Pauline was Irish Catholic. Harold's mother didn't want him to marry a girl of a different religion. Even some of his friends advised him not to marry someone who wasn't Jewish. Though Harold would have ignored this advice if he had been determined to marry Pauline, the young couple's romance didn't last. Whatever problems Harold's friends and relatives had with a marriage between the two, Pauline's friends and relatives mirrored those problems. As Catholics, many of them weren't happy with her marrying a non-Catholic. These attitudes could've been overcome, but Harold and Pauline were busy building careers. They had many interests besides each other.

While he was with the MacMaster company

1. *Los Olvidadoes*：《被遗忘的人们》(1950) 是西班牙导演路易斯·布努艾尔 (1900–1983) 的电影作品

数时间都在一起。演出间歇的日子，哈罗德带她去伦敦见父母。在伦敦，哈罗德带她去看电影。他仍旧是个电影迷。他们去看路易斯·布努艾尔执导的电影《被遗忘的人们》。布努艾尔执导了哈罗德最喜爱的电影之一——《一条安达鲁狗》。哈罗德钦佩布努艾尔的艺术风格。这位导演的艺术影响后来体现在哈罗德的写作和表演当中。

哈罗德的母亲喜欢保利娜，但又心存担忧——保利娜是爱尔兰天主教徒。哈罗德的母亲不想让他娶异教女孩。一些朋友甚至也建议他别娶非犹太女子。如果他执意要娶保利娜的话，哈罗德一定不会介意这些建议，不过这对年轻人的浪漫恋情好景不长。保利娜和哈罗德的亲友都有相同的担忧。作为天主教徒，许多人对她和非天主教徒结婚不高兴。这些态度本可克服，不过哈罗德和保利娜都忙于事业。除了彼此相恋外，各自都还有别的爱好。

和麦克马斯特剧团在爱尔兰期间，哈罗德还发现了对他写作影响最

in Ireland, Harold also found the writer who would have the greatest impact on his writing. He read, in *Poetry Ireland*, an excerpt from Samuel Beckett[1]'s novel, *Watt*. Beckett's style and subject matter excited him. Here was a writer whose art created a new literary world. Beckett's world, while odd to most readers, was one that Harold immediately recognized. Here was a literary world that Harold could feel at home in.

Ireland had given Harold Pinter many new experiences. He had played villains, detectives, and aristocrats. He had found a new love in Pauline Flanagan and a new literature in Samuel Beckett. His tour of Ireland gave him two years that he later said were "sometimes golden". After two years — five acting seasons — with the MacMaster company, however, he knew he needed to move on. To grow artistically, he reached out for new experiences.

In 1952, Harold started a novel, *The Dwarfs*, his autobiographical novel. This novel includes a character named Len. At least two men named Len had figured importantly in Harold's life up to that time. Len Hutton, the famous cricket player, was one of

1. Samuel Beckett: 塞缪尔·贝克特(1906－1989)，爱尔兰作家、戏剧家、诗人，荒诞派戏剧(Theatre of the Absurd)的代表人物之一，1969年诺贝尔文学奖得主，主要作品包括《等待戈多》(*Waiting for Godot*, 1952)等

大的作家。他在《爱尔兰诗歌》中读到塞缪尔·贝克特的小说《瓦特》的节选。贝克特的主题和风格令哈罗德感到兴奋。贝克特的艺术开创了文学新境界。虽然对大多数读者来说，贝克特的世界显得怪诞，但哈罗德看后马上能产生认同。这个文学世界让哈罗德找到了归属感。

爱尔兰给哈罗德带来了许多新体验。他在剧中扮演坏人、侦探和贵族。他发现了新的恋人保利娜·弗拉纳根和塞缪尔·贝克特的新式文学作品。爱尔兰巡演持续两年，他后来评价这段时间为"黄金时代"。在麦克马斯特剧团总计两年（五个演出季）后，哈罗德知道他得另谋出路了。为了艺术上的成长，他得去寻找新的经历。

1952年，哈罗德开始写自传体小说《侏儒》。小说中有个名为莱恩的人物。哈罗德的人生中，起码有两个叫莱恩的人对他产生过重要影响。其中一位是哈罗德童年时期的英雄、著名板球运动员莱恩·赫顿。另一

Harold's childhood heroes. Lennie, the retarded friend in John Steinbeck's *Of Mice and Men* had also made a deep impression on him. It was a name that had meaning for the young writer. It combined the physical world of sports and the imaginary world of fiction. After reading Beckett, Harold was more serious than ever about his writing. He kept at it even as he began a new acting job in London.

He joined Donald Wolfit's Shakespeare company for a three-month season. He soon found that Wolfit and MacMaster were quite different men to work for. MacMaster encouraged his actors to take on[1] new roles and responsibilities. In Harold's opinion, Wolfit did not. Wolfit seemed much less supportive of the actors in his company. He sometimes ridiculed his actors. He also expected actors to follow his instructions without question. MacMaster had been receptive to ideas from the actors.

During his three months with Donald Wolfit, Harold didn't move up the ladder to larger roles.

---

1. take on: *v.* 担当，肩负 (责任、义务)

位是约翰·斯坦贝克《鼠与人》中的智障朋友莱尼 (莱尼是莱恩的昵称)。这位智障的莱尼也对他产生了深远的影响。"莱恩"这个名字对这位年轻的作家有着特殊的意义，它将体育的物质世界和小说的假想世界合二为一了。读了贝克特的作品后，哈罗德写作更加认真了。即便后来在伦敦开始了新的演出工作，他仍笔耕不辍。

他参加了唐纳德·沃尔菲特莎士比亚剧团为期三个月的戏剧演出。他很快发现为麦克马斯特工作和为沃尔菲特工作大相径庭。麦克马斯特鼓励演员饰演新角色、承担新责任，而在哈罗德看来，沃尔菲特并非如此。他很少鼓励剧团中的演员，有时还会冷嘲热讽一番。他希望演员们言听计从，而麦克马斯特则能听取演员的想法。

在为唐纳德·沃尔菲特工作的三个月里，哈罗德未能更上一层楼，

He played in two ancient Greek tragedies: *Oedipus Rex*[1] and *Oedipus at Colonus*[2] In these plays, however, he had no leading part. He was in the chorus. His lines were spoken in unison[3] with others in the chorus.

Harold didn't get on with Wolfit as he had with MacMaster. Wolfit was authoritarian. Harold Pinter was never one to obey without asking questions. Wolfit didn't renew Pinter's contract. Wolfit didn't see Harold's talent as indispensable[4] to his company. Moreover, he was used to actors' ready and pleasant obedience to his wishes. Harold wasn't always the ready and pleasant sort.

Harold felt discouraged by Wolfit's rejection. He had to move back into his parents' house, but he didn't give up. He changed his stage name to David Baron and began looking for other acting jobs. While looking for acting jobs, he took odd jobs. Because he lived at home he could manage on the little bit of money he made as a waiter or shoveling[5] snow. He worked as a bouncer[6] in a bar for awhile. During this time he kept writing. He started a short story called "The Examination". He wrote new poems and continued working on *The Dwarfs*.

1. *Oedipus Rex*:《俄狄浦斯王》，古希腊索福克勒斯 (Sophocles, 公元前496-公元前406) 的悲剧之一
2. *Oedipus at Colonus*:《俄狄浦斯在科罗诺斯》，古希腊索福克勒斯的悲剧之一
3. in unison: 一致的，和谐的
4. indispensable: *adj.* 不可或缺的，必不可少的
5. shovel: *v.* 铲，铲除
6. bouncer: *n.* 保镖

去演主角。他出演了两部希腊悲剧——《俄狄浦斯王》和《俄狄浦斯在科罗诺斯》。不过，哈罗德在这些剧中没法演主角，他在合唱队里，台词是和合唱队里的其他人一起说的。

哈罗德和沃尔菲特相处得也不如和麦克马斯特那样融洽。沃尔菲特比较独断专行。哈罗德·品特不是那种只会服从、不作思考的人。沃尔菲特没有和他续约，他不觉得哈罗德有剧团不可或缺的才能。他也习惯了演员对他言听计从，而哈罗德则非俯首帖耳之辈。

沃尔菲特拒绝续约，哈罗德颇为沮丧。他搬回父母的房子，但是他并未就此放弃。他将艺名改为大卫·巴伦，并开始寻找其他演出机会。在此期间，他常去打零工。因为在家住，他能够设法用当服务生和铲雪赚的小钱来生活。他在酒吧做了一段时间保镖。他一直坚持写作，他开始写一篇题为《测验》的短篇小说，写新诗，并继续写《侏儒》。

During the next few years, Harold went from job to job and role to role without getting much critical attention for his acting abilities. During these years, however, he met the talented actress, Vivian Merchant, who *did* get critical acclaim for her work. At first the two young people didn't pay much attention to each other.

随后几年，哈罗德的工作换了一个又一个，演了一个又一个角色，但是他的演技并未获得多少关注。不过，那几年里，他遇到一位优秀的女演员维维恩·麦钱特，她的演出获得了评论界的好评。不过刚开始，这对年轻人并未留意对方。

Chapter Eight

A Start

事业起步

In the seaside town of Bournemouth[1], England, Harold performed in a different play each week, as he had in Ireland. His mother and father had honeymooned in Bournemouth, and it was there that he would get married.

He had met Vivien Merchant three years earlier, in 1953, when he was with Woolfit's acting troop. However, he hadn't gotten to know her well during that earlier time. This time would be different.

Vivien's birth name was Ada Thomson. She had adopted the stage name of Vivien Merchant because she liked Vivien Leigh — the actress and movie star — and because her brother was a merchant sailor. Vivien Merchant was only a year older than Harold, but she had much more acting experience. She'd started acting on stage when she was only fourteen years old. Now, in the Bournemouth productions, she was always given leading roles. She appealed to audiences because of her beauty as well as because of her talented acting.

The two young actors' jobs with the company threw them together constantly. They got to know each other better during rehearsals and found themselves more and more involved. At Bournemouth,

1. Bournemouth: 波恩茅斯，位于英格兰南部，是旅游胜地

在英格兰海滨小城波恩茅斯，同在爱尔兰一样，哈罗德每周在一部不同的戏中演出。他的父母曾在波恩茅斯度蜜月，那也是哈罗德后来结婚的地方。

三年前(1953年)，他在沃尔菲特的剧团时，遇到了维维恩·麦钱特。不过，那时候哈罗德对她了解不多。这次则不同。

维维恩出生时叫埃达·汤姆森。她喜欢电影明星费雯·丽(Vivien Leigh)，哥哥是商船(Merchant)水手，故取维维恩·麦钱特(Vivien Merchant)为艺名。维维恩·麦钱特只比哈罗德大一岁，演出经验却丰富许多，14岁时就已经登台表演。在波恩茅斯的演出中，她一直担任主角。她长相漂亮，演技精湛，很能吸引观众。

因工作关系，两个年轻人常在一起。彩排当中，他们逐渐了解对方，关系日渐亲密。波恩茅斯戏剧会演的第二部戏里，维维恩扮演简·爱——夏

in the second play of the season, Vivien played the role of Jane Eyre, heroine of Charlotte Bronte's famous story, *Jane Eyre*. Harold played Rochester, the hero. In the story, Jane falls in love with Rochester. Playing the part of lovers, they became lovers in real life.

The two decided to get married a few months after their acting company's season ended. They didn't want a formal, church wedding. On September 14, 1956, they went to the Bournemouth registry office, where they had a civil ceremony. They said their marriage vows to each other in front of the registry office supervisor. For their honeymoon, they went to Cornwall, not far from Caerhays Castle, where Harold had stayed as a boy.

Harold's parents weren't happy at his marrying a woman who wasn't Jewish. They were especially unhappy to learn that Harold had gotten married to a gentile[1] on an important Jewish holiday. Without realizing it, he had chosen Yom Kippur[2], for his wedding day. Yom Kippur is one of the most solemn Jewish holidays. It is a day for prayer and for repenting any wrong-doing. Harold's parents felt that his choosing that day to get married was an added insult to them. It added to the insult of

1. gentile: *n.* 非犹太人，异教徒，常译为 "外邦人"
2. Yom Kippur: *n.* 犹太人的赎罪日

洛特·勃朗蒂著名小说《简·爱》中的女主角，哈罗德扮演男主角罗切斯特。在戏里，简·爱与罗切斯特相爱。两个舞台上的恋人假戏真做，成了生活中的恋人。

剧团全演结束几个月后，二人决定结婚。他们不想办正式的教堂婚礼。1956 年 9 月 14 日，他们走进波恩茅斯婚姻登记处，在那里举办民事婚礼，在登记处官员面前宣誓结婚，接着去离卡尔海斯城堡不远的康沃尔度蜜月。

哈罗德的父母对他娶了个非犹太女子颇为不满。得知哈罗德在一个犹太教的重要节日娶了个外邦人，他们大为不悦。哈罗德忘了，把结婚日选在犹太教的赎罪日。赎罪日是最庄严的犹太节日之一，那天要做祷告，为做的错事忏悔。哈罗德的父母认为他选在赎罪日结婚是错上加错。本来，他拒绝娶犹太女人就是对他们的侮辱。尽管如此，他们最终还是

his refusing to marry a Jewish woman. However, they eventually forgave him for marrying a Catholic. He was their only son. They couldn't stay very angry with him.

After their wedding, Harold and Vivien went back to acting in repertory theater in the town of Torquay, in southwest England. Vivien always played leading roles. Harold was sometimes selected for leading parts, but he was often cast as a villain or a police inspector. Vivien devoted herself fully to acting. Harold worked hard at acting, too; but he devoted much of his time to his writing.

Only a couple of months later, in November, his devotion to writing was rewarded. While he and Vivien were at Torquay, Harold's career as a playwright got its start. Harold's friend, Henry Woolf, was studying drama in graduate school at Bristol University. The head of the Drama Department wanted to produce an evening of one-act plays. He wanted original plays that hadn't been copyrighted or performed yet. Henry immediately thought of his old friend, Harold Pinter. He wrote Harold a letter asking if he had written any one-act plays.

Harold hadn't. He sat down and wrote one as soon as he got Henry's letter. It took him four days. As soon as it was finished, he sent

原谅他娶了个天主教徒。他是父母的独子，他们不会一直生他的气。

婚礼之后，哈罗德和维维恩回到位于英国西南部小镇托凯的轮演剧院，继续演出。维维恩仍演主角，哈罗德演主角不多，反而经常被选去演恶棍或者警察局长。维维恩一心扑在演戏上。哈罗德同样努力演戏，但他大多数时间在写作。

几个月之后，在11月，他所迷恋的写作终于得到了回报。他和维维恩在托凯时，哈罗德的剧作家生涯开始了。哈罗德的朋友，亨利·伍尔夫正在布里斯托尔大学研究生院学习戏剧。戏剧系主任想制作一场晚间独幕剧，需要没有上演过且不存在版权问题的原创剧本。亨利立刻想到了他的老朋友哈罗德·品特，于是给哈罗德写了封信，问他是否写过独幕剧。

哈罗德没有写过。但他收到信后，立即坐下来动笔写。花了四天时

his script for "The Room" to Henry. Henry showed it to the head of the Drama Department, who liked the script and decided to use it.

"The Room", Harold Pinter's first play, was staged at Bristol the next spring, in May, 1958. Henry Woolf directed and acted in the play. Menacing and funny, the play showed influences from Samuel Beckett's work, especially his novel, *Murphy*. This play also started a sort of trademark for Pinter. This play, like many of his later plays, is set in one room. Like his later plays, "The Room" has only a few characters, all of whom are entangled[1] in a relationship that is odd, disturbing, and a little comic. Harold's hastily written play got good reviews in the Bristol newspaper.

Not long afterward, when Harold was staying overnight with a friend in Bristol, a literary agent came by late at night to meet him. The friend answered the door. The agent, Jimmy Wax, said he'd heard good things about "The Room" and would like to meet the playwright. Harold was in bed asleep when the agent arrived. He got out of bed and put on his robe. He and the friend he was visiting read a scene from the play aloud for the agent. The agent liked what he heard.

1. entangle: *v.* 纠缠，使混乱

向写了《房间》，写好后就寄给亨利。亨利把它拿给戏剧系主任，主任喜欢剧本并决定使用。

《房间》是哈罗德的首个剧本。翌年春天，即1958年5月，该剧在布里斯托尔被搬上舞台。亨利·伍尔夫执导该剧，并在剧中表演角色。该剧既恐怖又有趣，明显有塞缪尔·贝克特作品——尤其是小说《莫菲》——的痕迹。这部戏也开创了品特的招牌式风格。如他后来的许多戏剧一样，这部戏也发生在一个房间里。和后来的戏一样，《房间》里仅有少数几个角色，关系错综复杂。这些关系古怪离奇、令人不安，又有些滑稽。哈罗德仓促写成的戏获得了布里斯托尔报纸的好评。

不久，哈罗德在布里斯托尔一朋友处过夜，一个文学代理人深夜来访。朋友去应门。这位叫吉米·瓦克思的代理人说他获悉《房间》得到好评，想见见剧作者。哈罗德当时正在床上睡觉。他起床，穿上睡衣，和朋友一起向代理人读了剧中的一幕。代理人喜欢剧中的内容，向哈罗德

He asked Harold to let him act as his agent and try to sell the play to a publisher. Harold agreed. Jimmy Wax was now his agent — and he would be his agent for years, until Wax's death in 1983.

"The Room" was performed again in December 1957 at the National Student Drama Festival at Bristol University. The production was jointly produced by the drama department and the Bristol Old Vic Theatre School. This production won praise from an influential critic. He compared the play to Beckett's work and to the work of the great novelist, Henry James[1].

Such good reviews were important to Harold and his wife. Vivien was pregnant. Soon they would have a child to support. The couple lived in a basement, unable to pay their rent. Vivien did laundry to help make a living. Harold did other work, like stoking the furnace[2] in the building. They stayed worried and exhausted[3], but being young, they worked hard and hoped for better times.

Always short-tempered, Harold Pinter got into one of the few fistfights of his life. Having a drink,

1. Henry James: 亨利·詹姆斯 (1843-1916)，美国著名作家，19 世纪现实主义代表人物之一，开创了心理分析小说的先河，主要作品包括《美国人》(*The American*, 1877)、《贵妇人的肖像》(*The Portrait of a Lady*, 1881)、《金碗》(*The Golden Bowl*, 1904) 等
2. furnace: *n.* 炉子，火炉
3. exhaust: *v.* 使筋疲力尽，使疲惫

是否愿意让他做代理人，向出版商推销剧本。哈罗德答应了。吉米·瓦克恩成了哈罗德的代理人，这一代理就是几十年，直到 1983 年吉米逝世。

1957 年 12 月，《房间》在布里斯托尔大学举办的全国学生戏剧节上再次上演。此次演出是由布里斯托尔大学戏剧系和布利斯托尔老维克戏剧学院联袂演出的。演出得到了一位著名评论家的好评。他将《房间》和贝克特以及伟大的小说家亨利·詹姆斯的作品相提并论。

这些好评对哈罗德夫妇至关重要。维维恩怀孕了。不久两人家里就多了张嘴要喂了。夫妇俩住在地下室里，付不起租金。维维恩靠洗熨衣服谋生，哈罗德做着为楼房烧锅炉之类的杂活。他们很担心，也很疲惫，但他们都还年轻，都在努力工作，向往着好日子。

哈罗德·品特一直脾气暴躁，他一生很少打架，这期间却打了一次。他喝了点酒（喝酒是那段时间他仅有的几个奢侈爱好之一），哈罗德受到了

one of his few luxuries during this period, Harold suffered an insult
that was all too common to people of his background. A man in the bar
called him "a filthy Yid[1]". "Yid" is short for "Yiddish". This man's
insult to Pinter's Jewish background infuriated[2] him. He threw a punch
at the man. They began fighting. Someone in the bar called the police.
When the policeman arrived, he didn't arrest either Pinter or the other
man. He saw the fight as just a small disturbance. He also understood
Pinter's reasons for hitting the man. The murder of millions of Jews
during World War II showed with awful clarity the extremes of such
hatred.

By this time, Harold had written two more plays, "The Birthday
Party" and "The Dumb Waiter". "The Dumb Waiter" is another one-
act play. The title is a pun. It brings to mind a waiter who either cannot
speak or is stupid. It also brings to mind a shaft with a cart or elevator
for bringing food from the kitchen to another room.
This mechanism, which sometimes has a speaking
tube with it, figures as a part of the action in Pinter's
play about two hitmen who end up trying to kill
each other.

"The Birthday Party", which drew on some of

1. Yid: n. (谑称) 犹太人, 犹太
佬。Yid 是 Yiddish 的简写
2. infuriate: v. 激怒, 使狂怒

犹太背景的人常遇到的侮辱。酒吧里有人叫他"肮脏的犹佬"。"犹佬"
是"犹太佬"的简称。品特不堪其辱, 冲上去就是一拳, 两人对打起来。
酒吧有人叫来了警察。警察赶到后, 并未逮捕品特和另外那人。他把这
当做小事一桩。他了解品特打人的原因。二战中数百万犹太人遭到谋杀,
足见这一仇恨何等槽糕。

截至此时, 哈罗德又写了两部剧本,《生日晚会》和《送菜升降机》。
《送菜升降机》(The Dumb Waiter)是部独幕剧, 名字暗含双关, 既让人想
起不能说话或是笨(dumb)的服务生(waiter), 又让人想到厨房里的送菜升
降机(dumb waiter)。送菜升降机装置, 有时还带通话管, 它是戏剧动作
的一部分。戏中两个杀手最后都试图杀掉对方。

《生日晚会》部分取材于《房间》。该剧后来成为哈罗德最著名的作
品之一。1958年《生日晚会》首演, 获得了剑桥大学和牛津大学的好评。

the material of "The Room", would become one of his most famous works. First produced in 1958, it got good reviews in Cambridge and Oxford. However, when it was performed in London, at the Lyric Hammersmith Theater, the play flopped[1]. The reviews were terrible. Critics said they sat in the audience bored and confused by what happened on stage.

The bad reviews depressed everyone involved with the "The Birthday Party," from producer to actors to stagehands. Though the bad reviews dismayed Pinter as well, he didn't put much faith in critics' ability to tell a bad play from a good one. He had no serious thought of giving up playwriting. He had confidence in himself. His wife, Vivien, encouraged him. An experienced actress, she reminded him that bad reviews are simply a part of the life of any artist.

Then, just before "The Birthday Party" closed in London, Pinter got a break. A highly respected literary critic attended a matinee performance[2] of the play. The critic wrote a rave[3] review, proclaiming "The Birthday Party" a work of genius.

All of the years of writing led to this success. Harold Pinter's career as a playwright had begun.

1. flop: *v.* 失败，失利
2. matinee performance: *n.* (戏剧、电影的) 日场放映，日场演出
3. rave: *adj.* 非常热情的

不过，在伦敦利里克·哈默史密斯剧院上演时，却以失败告终。剧评十分负面，评论家说他们坐在观众席上，觉得台上的演出既无聊又费解。

负面剧评让制片人、演员、舞台管理以及与《生日晚会》有关的所有人都感到沮丧。品特自己也感到失望，但他并不完全相信评论家能区分戏剧的好坏。他没想过放弃剧本写作。他对自己有信心。妻子维维恩也给了他鼓励。作为经验丰富的女演员，她提醒哈罗德，劣评是艺术家生活的一部分。

随后，当《生日晚会》在伦敦演出结束前，品特缓了口气。一位极受尊敬的文学评论家参加了该剧的日场演出。这位评论家写了篇热情洋溢的剧评，声称《生日晚会》是部杰作。

这些年的一切努力终于造就了这次成功。哈罗德·品特作为戏剧家

He loved acting, and he would've liked to act in the famous Shakespeare productions at Stratford, England, or in the equally famous "Old Vic" playhouse in London. However, in spite of his strong stage presence and deep, resonant[1] voice, his unique talent wasn't in his roles on stage. His great gift was in creating the roles themselves for actors to perform. He wrote new worlds, strange ones, born out of the complex and turbulent[2] drama of his own life.

1. resonant: *adj.* 引起共鸣的
2. turbulent: *adj.* 狂暴的，动荡不安的

的职业生涯从此开始了。他热爱表演，喜欢在英格兰斯特拉福德剧院或者在同样知名的伦敦老维克剧场表演莎士比亚名剧。他有强烈的舞台表现力，有一副深沉、能引起共鸣的好嗓子，但他的独特才华并不体现在舞台上，而在于创造角色，让演员去演。他以自己那部复杂动荡的人生大戏为依托，创造了一个个新颖而古怪的戏剧世界。

Chapter Nine

Beginnings of Success and Failure

得意失意

That the bad reviews and early closing of "The Birthday Party" at the Lyric Hammersmith in London had thrown Pinter into a two-day slump[1] isn't surprising. He had gone to a cafe after the first performance to read the newspaper reviews of his play. On reading these, he briefly considered giving up on writing. As soon as Vivien reminded him that every artist gets some bad reviews, he regained his perspective[2]. Not only were critics often wrong about the merits or faults of a piece of art, audiences were often wrong, too. He knew that the main person he ought to please was himself. Because of his own self confidence and Vivien's unwillingness to grant him an excuse to be depressed, he pulled out[3] of his depression quickly. He took acting jobs and kept writing, all the while seeking producers for his plays and publishers for his poems. He also continued to do work around the building they lived in, serving as caretaker since they couldn't pay the rent for their dingy basement rooms in Notting Hill Gate, a shabby[4] section of London. Vivien did less laundry as she neared the end of her pregnancy. In their dismal apartment, the couple awaited the birth of their first child.

Their son Daniel was born on January 19, 1958.

1. slump: *n.* 低潮，消沉
2. perspective: *n.* 恰当的观点
3. pull out: *v.* 渡过难关
4. shabby: *adj.* 破败的，破旧的

《生日晚会》劣评如潮，在伦敦利里克·哈默斯剧院的上演又提前结束，哈罗德为此足足消沉了两天，这一反应一点也不奇怪。首演结束后，他在咖啡馆里读到《生日晚会》的剧评。读罢，他考虑是否就此金盆洗手，不再写作了。维维恩提醒他，每位艺术家都会遇到负面评论，这话让哈罗德的心态恢复了正常。不单是评论家常会误评作品，观众也常犯错。他知道该取悦的人是自己。出于自信，加之维维恩也不给他有沮丧的借口，哈罗德很快摆脱了消沉。他继续出演角色，坚持写作，同时为剧本和诗歌寻找制片人和出版商。他也继续在住处附近工作，自从付不起伦敦破败街区诺丁山门地下室的租金后，他一直做看门人。维维恩因为产期临近，洗衣服少了。在阴郁的公寓里，夫妇俩等着第一个孩子的降生。

他们的儿子丹尼尔生于 1958 年 1 月 19 日。在医院，维维恩难产，经

In the hospital, Vivien had a terribly difficult labor[1], so difficult that she never wanted to have any more children.

Upset at the thought of his wife and child living in the basement, Pinter wrote to a woman who admired Vivien's acting. He told her that he and his wife couldn't afford a decent apartment. The woman sent money so they could rent a nicer one. This kindness from a fan of Vivien's meant that the three could move to a brighter, healthier place. Harold and Vivien never forgot this kindness.

While Vivien recovered from childbirth and took care of baby Daniel, Pinter took what acting jobs he could get. When he was home, he wrote, using ideas and images from his life, as every author does. Sometimes he used images from childhood, sometimes from more recent experiences.

For "The Birthday Party", he had borrowed from something that happened to him in 1954, when he'd had a very minor role — working the head piece of a mechanical stage horse — while touring with a play called, "A Horse! A Horse!" According to Michael Billington, who wrote the first major biography of Pinter, the playwright used material he stored away in memory from a house where he stayed during

1. difficult labor: n. 难产

此一劫，她都不想再生小孩了。

品特对妻儿住在地下室忧心仲仲，于是写信给一位喜爱维维恩表演的女士，信中说他们没钱租更好的公寓。这位女士当即寄来钱，让他们能够租向条件好点的公寓。托维维恩戏迷的福，他们三人能够搬进更明亮、更健康的住处。哈罗德和维维恩一直忘不了这份好意。

在维维恩生月子和照顾小丹尼尔期向，哈罗德什么演出的活都干。在家里，同其他作家一样，他用生活中的想法和意象来写作。有时他用童年的意象，有时则用最近的经历。

写《生日晚会》时，他借用了 1954 年发生的事。他们巡演剧目中包含一出名为《马！马！》的戏，品特在其中扮演配角，主要任务就是操纵一个机械马的头部。据品特第一部主要传记作者迈克尔·比林顿介绍，品特根据记忆，以此次巡演期向住的一向房子为素材创作了剧本。一天晚上演出结束后，品特在一向酒吧里喝酒，正考虑晚上住哪里。酒吧里

this tour. One night after the show, Pinter went to have a drink in a pub and decide where to spend the night. He met a man there who told him about a cheap place to stay. Pinter went with the man and rented a bed in the house, which was dirty and unkempt[1]. He followed the man upstairs to an attic room. The landlady was a big woman and her husband, the landlord, a little man. During his stay, Pinter saw the woman make rough, boldly flirtatious[2] gestures toward the man whom Pinter had met in the pub. She tousled[3] the man's hair at the supper table. She tickled him when he tried to tell her something. The man didn't seem to like it, but he didn't say anything to the woman. These characters formed the outlines of three of the main characters in Pinter's 1957 play.

In "The Birthday Party", Pinter introduces two additional characters, named Goldberg and McCann. These two are the villains of the play. They come to the house and within only a short time render Stanley — the roomer — almost mute. They break his glasses and, in the end, take him away against his will. Goldberg and McCann have been thought to represent the Jewish and Catholic faith. They're oppressive[4] in the play, taking away Stanley's voice and vision as well as what freedom he had. However, the playwright doesn't

1. unkempt: *adj.* 蓬乱的，不整洁的
2. flirtatious: *adj.* 调戏的，娇媚的
3. tousle: *v.* 弄乱，搅乱
4. oppressive: *adj.* 压制的，压迫的

有个人告诉他有个便宜的住处。品特随着那人走到一所肮脏零乱的房子，并在那里租了个床位。他跟着男人走上阁楼。女房东身材高大，而她的丈夫（房东）则身材瘦小。居住期间，品特看到，女房东跟他在酒吧里遇到的那男子毫无顾忌地调情。晚餐时，她在桌上弄乱那男人的头发。当他想说话时，她逗笑他。这个男人似乎不喜欢这样，但也未对她说什么。这些人物构成了品特1957年戏剧里的三个主要人物。

《生日晚会》中，品特还添加了两个人物，戈德堡和麦凯恩。他们是剧里的恶棍。他们闯入房子，很快就把房客斯坦利逼迫得几乎成了哑巴。他们打坏他的眼镜，最终强行将他带走。戈德堡和麦凯恩被当作是犹太教和天主教的象征，在剧中具有压迫性，他们夺走了斯坦利的声音和视

create them as thoroughly villainous; they too, seem to be at the mercy of[1] some larger force that limits their own freedom. Pinter had turned away from the Jewish religion. He didn't care for the Catholic religion either. He knew, however, that Jews and Irish-Catholics had been the victims of persecution[2] themselves.

While Vivien fed the baby or put him to bed, she often heard her husband reading lines aloud. He always read his work aloud when he was writing a play. Both of them continued to worry about money.

This worry took a toll[3] on both of them, but in different ways. Vivien cared for the baby almost constantly. She mashed up[4] baby food. She changed diapers. She got up in the night to give the baby milk. She faced many problems, but in having a baby and taking good care of it, she was at least successful in the important role of mother. At that time in England, men were expected to be the family's main source of financial support. Harold felt himself a failure in the role of father. To be responsible for a wife and baby caused him more stress than he knew.

Harold woke up from a dream one night in tears. Vivien awoke too and sat up in bed.

1. at the mercy of: 任由某人／某物摆布或控制
2. persecution: n. 烦扰，迫害
3. take a toll: 造成损失，破坏
4. mash up: v. 将某物捣成糊状

力，也剥夺了他的自由。不过，品特并未把他们写成十恶不赦的恶棍。他们自己也受制于一些更强大的力量，这些力量限制着他们的自由。品特已经放弃了犹太教，他也不在乎天主教。他知道犹太人和爱尔兰天主教徒都是宗教迫害的受害者。

维维恩喂孩子或是哄他上床时，常听见哈罗德大声读台词。他创作剧本时，总是大声朗读作品。他俩仍为钱担忧。

这个担忧对他们都有不良影响，只是方式不同。维维恩几乎一直在照料孩子：将婴儿食品做成糊，给孩子换尿布，半夜起身喂奶。她面临很多问题，但是生孩子照顾孩子，起码会有做母亲的成就感。那时在英国，男人是家庭的主要经济来源。哈罗德感到作为一位父亲自己很失败。对妻儿的责任给他带来的压力比预想的大得多。

一天晚上，哈罗德从梦中哭着醒来。维维恩也被吵醒，坐在床上。

"What's wrong?" she asked sleepily, concerned, but grumpy[1] at being awakened. She was awakened in the night by the baby often enough. Now here was her husband waking her up.

At first Harold didn't really know why he was crying. He looked over at their six-month-old baby, sleeping in the small cot nearby.

"What's going to happen to him?" he asked his wife suddenly. He realized that the sadness he felt was the heavy weight of worry about his son. Having lived through the blitz, he knew the terrors of bombs dropping from the sky. He knew the dangers life held — war, illness, accident, and crime. Even the ordinary pressures of earning a living and providing for a family could be overwhelming. All of those problems and the universal human awareness of his or her own death, Harold dreaded for his son. Daniel lay there, tiny and innocent. Dread bore down on[2] Harold. He could face up to these problems himself, but the idea of his infant son's having to face them was too much for him at that moment.

To make some extra money, he answered an ad asking for people to be tested in a research program. Harold agreed to be a subject in the experiment. He went the institute and was put in a chair. After checking Harold's blood pressure, a doctor put earphones

1. grumpy: *adj.* 脾气坏的，脾气暴躁的
2. bore down on (sb/sth): *v.* 向某人/某物迅速逼近

"怎么了？"她带着倦意和担忧问道，但是睡得好好的被吵醒她还是多少有些恼恼。她常被孩子吵醒，现在又给丈夫吵醒了。

刚开始哈罗德也不知道自己为什么哭。他看着六个月大的儿子，正睡在一边的小婴儿床里。

"他会怎么样？"他突然问妻子。他意识到自己的悲伤源自对儿子深深的忧虑。他经历过闪电战，知道天上掉炸弹的恐怖，知道生活的危险——战争、疾病、事故和罪行，甚至养家糊口的压力都叫人不堪承受。这些问题，以及人类对死亡的普遍担忧，哈罗德为儿子忧心忡忡。幼小的丹尼尔就睡在那里，浑然不知世事。这担忧都郁积在哈罗德身上。他自己尚可面对这些问题，但是儿子将如何面对，此时此刻，这个想法让他倍感压力。

为了多赚钱，他按一广告的指引，参加了一个研究项目，同意做实验对象。他去研究所，坐在椅子上。检查血压后，医生给他戴上耳机，

on him and attached electrodes[1] to him. He sat there. Suddenly, a loud noise came over the earphones. His heart thumped[2] loudly.

"Quite startling, wasn't it?" commented the doctor, removing the earphones and electrodes. He told Harold they were testing people's reactions to noise. He didn't say what the purpose of the experiment was or how the results would be used, however. Harold collected his money for this strange job and left.

Luckily, he had some admirers of his writing. "The Birthday Party" was revived as a play. Supporters of his in the British Broadcasting Corporation[3]'s radio and television divisions asked him to submit[4] plays to them. His play "A Slight Ache", written in response to a request from BBC radio, features a bad marriage. The couple in the play can't agree about much of anything, including how to kill a wasp[5] that has gotten into the house. Vivien can't have been pleased with his choice of subject. However, the play was successful. "The Birthday Party" was produced for BBC television. At this point, chances for Harold's success in a writing career were improving.

However, at the same time that he began to have some real suc-

1. electrodes: n. 电极
2. thump: v. 砰砰响，重击
3. British Broadcasting Corporation: 英国广播公司，简称BBC，是英国政府资助但独立运作的媒体，全球最受尊敬的媒体之一
4. submit: v. 提交，递交
5. wasp: n. 黄蜂

贴上电极。他坐在那里，突然耳机里一阵噪音，他的心怦怦作响。

"很吓人吧，是不？"医生问道，一边移去耳机和电极。他告诉哈罗德他们在测试人对噪音的反应。不过，他并未说出实验的目的和实验结果的用途。哈罗德拿到钱后就走了，离开了这个奇怪的差事。

很幸运，他的作品有人欣赏。《生日晚会》又重新上演。哈罗德在英国广播公司(BBC)广播电视分部的支持者们请他提交剧本。《微痛》就是哈罗德应BBC的请求而作的，讲的是失败婚姻的故事。剧中的夫妇几乎就所有问题都不能达成一致，包括如何杀死一只飞进房间的黄蜂。维维恩对他的选题可能不大开心。不过，剧本却很成功。《生日晚会》被拍成BBC电视剧。此时，哈罗德的写作事业看来在走上坡路。

事业上刚获得一些实质上的成功，他的婚姻就遇到了问题。他和维

cess in his career, he began to have trouble in his marriage. Neither he nor Vivien felt as happy as when they'd gotten married. Vivien seemed grouchy[1]. She complained about Harold's writing plays about some of his experiences and about people he knew. She thought this was unfair and disloyal. She wanted the two of them to go on tour acting rather than stay in London. To go would've suited her acting career. To stay suited his writing career. They stayed in London. Even though Harold was making a name for himself as Harold Pinter, the playwright, Vivian still called him "David" — as she did for the rest of her life.

In calling him by the stage name, "David Baron", he'd used when they'd worked together in Torquay, she seemed to want to keep him in the same role he'd been when they first met. One problem in their marriage was that, while she was still "Vivien" and acting was still her vocation[2], he was really no longer "David". Another was that he could more easily pursue his writing career at home with a new baby than she could pursue her acting career. Instead of bringing them closer together, their lack of money, their new baby, and their hopes for the future were creating a gulf between them.

1. grouchy: *adj.* 不高兴的，不满的
2. vocation: *n.* 职业，事业

维恩都不像刚结婚时那样恩爱了。维维恩看起来很不开心。她抱怨哈罗德的写作写入了他的亲身经历和他知道的人。她认为这既不公平也不忠诚。她想两人去巡回演出，而不是一直呆在伦敦。离开伦敦对她的演出事业有好处，留下来则对哈罗德的写作有益。他们选择了呆在伦敦，即使哈罗德作为戏剧家哈罗德·品特的声誉日隆，维维恩却仍叫他"大卫"——她后来还一直这么叫他，一辈子未曾改口。

"大卫·巴伦"是哈罗德在托凯演出时的艺名，维维恩叫他这个名字，表明她似乎希望哈罗德停留在他们最初见面时的那个角色中。他们婚姻的问题之一，是她没变，仍是演员"维维恩"，而哈罗德已今非昔比，不再是"大卫"了。另一个问题是家里多了个孩子，哈罗德仍能呆在家从事写作，她却无法在家里演出。夫妇俩缺钱，多了个小孩，又对未来充满期望，但这些并没有将双方拉近，反而成为他们之间的巨大鸿沟。

Chapter Ten

PINTERESQUE

品特风格

"The Caretaker", Pinter's next play, brought him the success he'd hoped for. First performed in April, 1960, by the Arts Theater Club in London, it played for a month there. Because of its success, the play opened in the Duchess Theater in London's West End right after its close at the Arts Theater Club. "The Caretaker" was a big hit[1] with reviewers. It won a major award as the best play of 1960. Never again would Pinter go to a theater to find only six people sitting in the audience, as he had on a Thursday matinee[2] performance of "The Birthday Party" at the Lyric Hammersmith theatre.

This success, however, had a bad effect on his marriage. His wife, Vivien, had helped him through bad reviews and hard times. She had lived with him in the ugly little basement apartment where he'd written "The Caretakers", in 1959. She'd been a caretaker with him in the apartment building they'd lived in. Yet she did not completely share in his good fortune.

1. hit: *n.* 风靡一时的事物
2. matinee: *n.* 日场表演，日场音乐会

Pinter was able to continue writing through their hard times partly because of Vivien's willingness to stay in London when she could've had acting jobs elsewhere. She also took on most of the job of caring for their son. Pinter continued to act until

品特的下一部剧作《看门人》带来了他所渴望的成功。《看门人》最早于1960年4月在伦敦艺术剧院俱乐部上演，演出持续一个月。由于演出大获成功，在艺术剧院俱乐部演出结束后，又在伦敦西区公爵夫人剧院上演。《看门人》受到评论家的热烈欢迎，获得了1960年度最佳戏剧奖。情形再不会像利里克·哈默史密斯剧院的《生日晚会》星期四日场表演那样，当品特走进剧院发现只有六名观众了。

不过，这次成功却对他的婚姻产生了不良影响。维维恩和他携手走过劣评，渡过难关，两人曾一起住在脏乱的小地下室。就在1959年，两人都为公寓看门的时候，品特在那地下室写下了《看门人》。可是当品特有福了，维维恩却不能同享。

品特能在困难时期继续写作，部分是因维维恩愿意呆在伦敦。她本可以到其他地方去演出。她承担了照料儿子的大部分工作。品特一直表演到1959年，在妻子的演出收入外增添了自己的一份收入。他们为着全

1959, adding his acting income to his wife's. They both worked to earn a living for themselves and their baby. They couldn't go on long acting tours, however, and stayed in London where Harold needed to be to get his scripts performed.

In 1959, Pinter quit acting for a living. He devoted almost all of his time to writing and promoting his plays. He wrote "The Caretaker" that year, sitting at his desk, trying to think and type, with Daniel crawling underfoot. However, Vivien didn't let the baby be too much of a bother. She picked him up and changed his diapers, fed him, played with him, and put him to bed at night.

They needed money badly. Vivien was glad that her husband's success meant more income. The additional money would make their lives more comfortable. She was especially glad when she thought of their son, Daniel.

However, her feelings about his success were mixed, for several reasons. One reason had to do with his new play. She had an objection to Pinter's way of getting material for his plays. He created characters from people he knew in real life. She thought this was not a good thing to do, especially when he portrayed the characters in an unflattering[1] way. She hated "The Caretaker" because she thought it was unfair to the

> 1. unflattering: *adj.* 不讨好人 的，不奉承人的

家努力工作。不过，他们不能长期外出巡回演出，只得呆在伦敦。哈罗德只有在伦敦，才能将自己的剧本搬上舞台。

1959 年，品特放弃了演出这一谋生之路，几乎将全时间投入到写作和推销剧本上。写《看门人》那年，他坐在桌边，一边思考一边打字，丹尼尔就在他脚下爬。不过，维维恩不让孩子过多打扰品特。她把孩子抱起来，给他换尿布、喂奶、陪他玩，晚上哄他上床睡觉。

他们急需钱用。丈夫的成功意味着更多的收入，这让维维恩感到高兴。多些钱日子会好过些。想到儿子丹尼尔，她就特别开心。

不过，她对哈罗德的成功感觉复杂，原因有几条。一是和新戏有关。她对品特戏剧的取材方式有异议。品特从真实生活中创造人物。她认为这样做不对，尤其是品特下笔不大恭敬的时候。她讨厌《看门人》。她觉得这对真实生活中的人有失公允。她特别讨厌品特笔下阿斯顿这个人

real people it was based on. She particularly disliked Pinter's character of Aston. The man on whom this character was based had been nice to the couple and their baby. Austin — the man's name — was the brother of the man who owned the apartment building Harold and Vivien lived in. Austin had been impressed that Harold was a writer. He even installed a telephone in their apartment building when he learned that Harold needed to talk to people about getting his plays performed. In "The Caretaker", Aston is portrayed as mentally retarded and in need of care from his older brother. This portrayal would have insulted both brothers if they knew about it. Austin, had indeed been in a mental institution, as has Aston in the play. Austin had also had electric shock therapy. Vivien disliked Pinter's use of the man's problems in a play for the public, even if the man never learned about it. She thought Pinter's use of knowledge about Austin was a little heartless[1].

The character of Aston is unflattering to the man who inspired it, but it's not much less flattering than the characters of Mick and Davies, who are also based on men Pinter met in the apartment building where he lived. The owner of the building is Mick in the play. He's intelligent enough, but crude and unsympathetic. When Aston brings a homeless man home to give him a place to stay for a night or two, Mick doesn't like it. Aston regrets it too. The man, based on a homeless

1. heartless: *adj.* 无情的

物。阿斯顿的原型对品特夫妇和孩子很好。此人真名奥斯汀——是哈罗德和维维恩居住的公寓房主的弟弟。奥斯汀听说哈罗德是作家，对他肃然起敬。得知哈罗德因排戏要和人联系，他特地在公寓里装了部电话。而在《看门人》中，阿斯顿被描写成需要哥哥照顾的智障。这种描写全侮辱这对兄弟。如同剧中的阿斯顿一样，奥斯汀确实住过精神病院，还接受过电击治疗。不管原型是否知晓，维维恩讨厌品特将个人隐私在戏剧中公之于众的做法。她认为品特如此运用奥斯汀的故事有些无情无义。

剧中的阿斯顿贬低了人物原型，不过米克和戴维斯这两角色的情形也差不多。这两位原型和品特曾同住一幢公寓楼。公寓主人在戏中成了米克。他倒是不笨，不过很粗俗，没有同情心。阿斯顿把无家可归者带

man that Austin really did bring to the building, stayed almost a month before he was made to leave. This third character is Davies in the play. He is deceitful and disloyal. The most admirable trait of all three characters is that they survive despite their circumstances.

"The Caretakers" is set in an unkempt attic room in which nothing much happens other than Davies's half-hearted[1] knife threat against Aston and a funny struggle over a bag full of Davies's worthless belongings. Several earlier playwrights had prepared audiences for this new type of serious, but comical drama. "The Caretakers" is in the tradition of the "theater of the absurd[2]". This type of drama began after World War II. It seems to come from a modern cynicism[3] about people's ability to relate to each other or the world around them. Some historians believe this attitude results from the horrors of World War II. However, the increasing mechanization of many of society's functions inspired this

1. half-hearted: *adj.* 缺乏热情的，半心半意的
2. theater of the absurd: 荒诞派戏剧，20世纪50年代兴起于法国的反传统戏剧流派。1950年法国剧作家尤奈斯库 (Eugène Ionesco, 1909–1994) 的《秃头歌女》(*La Cantatrice Chauve*) 问世，1953年贝克特又以剧作《等待戈多》(*En attendant Godot*) 轰动法国舞台，1961年英国批评家艾思林 (Martin Esslin, 1918–2002) 发表《荒诞派戏剧》(*Theatre of the Absurd*) 一书，将这类作品作了理论上的概括，并正式命名。此后，荒诞派戏剧达到成熟和全盛。荒诞派戏剧家提倡纯粹戏剧性、通过直喻把握世界，他们放弃了形象塑造与戏剧冲突，运用支离破碎的舞台直观场景、奇特怪异的道具、颠三倒四的对话、混乱不堪的思维，表现现实的丑恶与恐怖、人生的痛苦与绝望，达到一种抽象的荒诞效果。代表作家有尤奈斯库、贝克特、品特等
3. cynicism: *n.* 悲观厌世的，玩世不恭的

回公寓，想留宿一两晚，米克却不同意，阿斯顿也感到很遗憾。而奥斯汀带回来的那个无家可归者，却在公寓里住了将近一个月。第三个人物戴维斯在剧中奸诈且不忠诚。剧中三个人物最令人钦佩的品质是能在恶劣的环境里活下来。

《看门人》以零乱的阁楼为背景，情节平淡，唯一不平淡之处是戴维斯半真半假地拿刀子威胁阿斯顿，以及他们为了戴维斯一袋子不值钱的东西发生了滑稽的打斗。先前一些剧作家已经让观众有所准备，能接受这种亦庄亦谐的新型戏剧——"荒诞派戏剧"。这类戏剧始于二战以后，似乎源自现代人对相互交往的能力以及与周遭世界之关系的嘲讽。一些历史学家认为这种嘲讽出自

tradition as well.

Futility[1] is an important element of this tradition, as is persistence[2] in spite of the apparent futility of struggle. The comedy in Pinter's and other absurdist playwrights is a kind of bleak comedy. It gets the audience to laugh at the poor logic and ineffectualness[3] of the characters. None of the characters is heroic in the classic sense. They are ordinary people, even "small" in terms of their limited perspectives on their situation. They are so intellectually small and their confinement[4] so tight, that they put some audiences in mind of characters on television. Early televisions had small screens and were in black and white, rather than color. Television itself confines its viewers. While people listening to a radio can walk around the room or even leave the room and still hear the radio, people who watch television usually have to sit in the room and stare at the screen. Mechanization of entertainment, through radio and television, meant it could go on all day long. It tempted people to relate less to each other and to do less active things inside or outside. With radio and television and more routine work, people seemed to be becoming more isolated from each other and the world around them.

1. futility: *n.* 无益，无用
2. persistence: *n.* 坚持，持续
3. ineffectualness: *n.* 无效，不成功
4. confinement: *n.* 局限，限制，禁锢

对二战的恐惧。不过，许多社会功能日益机械化的倾向也激发了该传统。

该传统的一个要素是徒劳感，另一要素是明知抗争徒劳却坚持不懈的精神。品特和其他荒诞派剧作家的作品属于灰色喜剧。它让观众为人物的不合逻辑和人物行动的徒劳而发笑。这些人物都不是经典意义上的英雄，他们是普通人。他们是小人物，对自己的处境知之甚少。他们并不机智，也受诸多局限，让观众想起电视机里的人物。早期的电视是小屏幕的黑白电视。电视机本身就局限了观众。人们听广播时还能在房间里走来走去，甚至离开房间也能听，而电视观众通常只能坐在那里盯着荧屏。广播和电视让娱乐变得机械化，它们能持续一整天，让人不再交流，不再活跃于室内或室外。广播电视的普及以及日常工作的日渐程式化，也让人们相互隔绝，让人与周遭世界也日趋隔绝。

The hardships of war, the dubious[1] comfort of mass entertainment twenty-four hours a day, seven hours a week, and the increased mechanization of work all contributed to making people feel that inhuman forces had control of their lives — and not the mostly benevolent[2] God or gods that had seemed to rule in the centuries before.

"The Caretaker" like most of Pinter's plays has characters who behave strangely. However, his characters and plot are fairly realistic. This play, like most of his others, isn't as "absurd" or bizarre as many plays in this genre. It is set in Hackney, Pinter's childhood neighborhood. It is believable as something that could happen in a rundown[3] building there. Combining absurdities and realism, this play appealed to a wider audience than many plays in the tradition of the theatre of the absurd. "The Caretaker" had a run of over four hundred performances at the Duchess Theater in London's West End. It has been performed many times since it opened. It remains his most popular play.

With the success of this play, rather suddenly Vivien's husband was *the* Harold Pinter, brilliant playwright. There was no female role in this play,

1. dubious: *adj.* 可疑的，怀疑的
2. benevolent: *adj.* 慈善的，仁慈的
3. rundown: *adj.* 破败的，破损的，年久失修的

战争令人生活困顿，大众媒体一年到头给人灌迷魂汤，工作也越来越机械化，这一切使人们感到冥冥之中有什么力量在控制着自己，这力量不是多半情况下比较仁慈的上帝，或是更早的那些神祇。

《看门人》和品特的其他戏剧一样，人物举止怪诞。不过，品特的人物和情节非常现实。和品特的大多数戏一样，这部戏并不像大部分"荒诞派戏剧"那样"荒诞"。它们以品特童年的社区哈克尼为背景，很可信，仿佛就发生在那里任何一个破败的楼房里。该剧结合了荒诞和现实主义，比许多典型的荒诞派戏剧吸引了更多的观众。《看门人》在伦敦西区公爵夫人剧院上演了四百余场，久演不衰，至今仍是品特最受欢迎的剧作之一。

随着戏剧的成功，维维恩的丈夫转眼间成了杰出戏剧家哈罗德·品特。《看门人》剧中没有女性角色，但是维维恩在哈罗德的第一部戏《房

but Vivien had acted in a production of "The Room", his first play. She had also acted in another play of his, "A Slight Ache", a play based on his brief boyhood stay in the countryside during the blitz. As an actress in his plays, she acted out lines he'd written. Having these roles was a benefit to her. But, viewed in another way, she was submitting her talent to his. She had become one of the many wives of the time who found her career hindered[1] by marriage and motherhood. Much as she loved her son and however much she loved her husband, in only three or four years, in their marriage and in their careers, she found herself playing a supporting role to his lead. His success surpassed[2] hers.

That summer, they moved to a suburban house in Kew, at the edge of London. They had more money than they'd ever had. Harold surprised Vivien with one idea about how to spend their money.

"But, a *car*, David?" Vivien asked. "You can't even drive!"

London had plenty of public transportation. A car was a luxury, but Harold wanted one anyway.

"I can learn, can't I? Until then, you can drive us," Harold argued. Vivien knew how to drive a car already.

---

1. hinder: *v.* 阻碍，阻止
2. surpass: *v.* 超越，胜过

向》里出演了一个角色。她也曾在哈罗德的戏《微痛》里演出。这部戏讲的是闪电战期间哈罗德在乡间短暂停留的故事。作为剧中的女演员，她绕着哈罗德写的台词。饰演这些角色对她很有好处。但是从另一个角度看来，她是为了哈罗德委屈了自己的才能。和当时诸多女性一样，她发现自己的事业受到婚姻和母亲身份的阻碍。她爱儿子，更爱丈夫，但婚后的三四年当中，在婚姻和事业上，她发现自己成了丈夫的配角。哈罗德胜过了她。

那年夏天，他们搬到伦敦郊区一个叫"邱"的地方住。他们的钱比以往都多。哈罗德想了个花钱的主意，这让维维恩感到吃惊。

"什么，买辆车，大卫？"维维恩问道。"你还不会开车！"

伦敦公交设施健全。汽车是奢侈品，但是哈罗德还是想买一辆。

"我可以学，不是吗？到那时，你也可以开，"哈罗德辩解道。维维恩那时已经会开车了。

A car was a status symbol[1]. It showed Harold's success. Vivien had mixed feelings about it. It would give her more freedom, but it would also mean she couldn't stay home if Harold needed to be driven somewhere — at times, to cricket matches, which he loved and she hated.

Vivien took a down-to-earth[2], anti-intellectual stance[3] toward literature. She valued practicality. She thought a lot of what was said about her husband's plays was simply rubbish, made up of fancies. When people started calling the use of long pauses in a play's dialog "Pinteresque[4]", she laughed. Silences and pauses were certainly important in Pinter's plays, as they are in all plays. Because of the inarticulateness[5] of the characters in his plays, silences were especially important. Still, she thought their significance in his work was overblown by the critics and fans. Even Pinter thought the designation[6] "Pinteresque" a little silly. He felt flattered by it, nevertheless. At times it seemed that the more appreciation he got from other people, the less appreciation he got from his wife.

1. status symbol: *n.* 社会地位的象征
2. down-to-earth: *adj.* 实际的，不加渲染的
3. stance: *n.* 姿态，立场
4. Pinteresque: *adj.* 品特风格，品特风格的戏剧
5. inarticulateness: *n.* 口齿不清的，说话不连贯的
6. designation: *n.* 名称，定名

汽车是社会地位的象征，它显示了哈罗德的成功。维维恩对其感觉复杂。汽车会给她更多自由，但是这意味着如果哈罗德想去什么地方，她就没法呆在家里——比如品特有时会去看他喜欢的板球赛，而维维恩则很讨厌这种运动。

维维恩对文学抱有一种实用、反智的立场。她欣赏实用性。她认为对哈罗德戏剧的评论大部分都是垃圾，是凭空臆想。当人们开始将戏剧对话中使用大段停顿称作"品特风格"时，她会笑起来。沉默和停顿在哈罗德的戏剧或是所有戏剧中都很重要。因为哈罗德戏剧中的人物说话不清楚，沉默就至关重要。不过，她认为这些沉默和停顿受到评论家和戏迷的过分吹捧。甚至连品特自己都认为"品特风格"这个名称有些愚蠢。不过，他感到很受用。有时，似乎他从其他人那得到的赞誉越多，从妻子嘴里得到的赞誉就越少。

Chapter Eleven

NEW HOMES AND THE HOMECOMING

新家与归家

n 1963, because of Pinter's success with "The Caretaker" and other works, he was able to buy a house in Worthing, a seaside town. Many of their theater friends were surprised by this choice. Worthing is a two-hour drive from London. It's a pleasant, cozy[1] town, with many older people living there. To the Pinters' friends, it seemed too staid[2] and out of the way[3]. However, it looked like a good town to raise their child in. It also afforded peace and quiet so that Harold could write.

Pinter and his family moved into a handsome, bow-fronted Regency[4] house on Ambrose Place in Worthing. The house was roomy[5] and comfortable. After they settled in, Daniel got a pet cat. When Daniel's cat got stuck on the roof one day and couldn't get down, the firemen who came to rescue the cat were glad to come. In such a calm little town, they didn't have many fires to put out. Not many emergencies of other types occupied their time either.

Joseph Brearley, Harold's teacher from high school, came to visit him in his new home by the sea. As always, Harold was getting a lot of writing done. In fact, one reason he was glad to see Brearley

1. cozy: *adj.* 舒适的，惬意的
2. staid: *adj.* 沉静的，安静地
3. out of the way: *adj.* 偏僻的，偏远的
4. Regency: *n.* 英国历史上的摄政时期（1810–1830）
5. roomy: *adj.* 宽敞的，宽大的

1963年，因《看门人》和其他戏剧的成功，品特得以在海滨小镇沃辛买了座房子。许多戏剧界朋友为这个选择感到吃惊。沃辛距伦敦有两小时车程，是个舒适宜人的小镇，镇上住着不少老年人。品特的朋友们觉得沃辛过于沉静和偏僻。不过，那里倒是个抚养孩子的好地方，也为哈罗德提供了一个安静的写作场所。

品特一家搬进了沃辛安布罗斯广场附近一所摄政时期风格的房子。房子有弓形的前门，漂亮、宽敞、舒适。他们安顿下来后，丹尼尔养了只猫。有一天猫跑到屋顶上下不来，消防员很乐于前来营救猫。在这样一个安宁的小城，火灾不常发生，也没有多少紧急事件。

哈罗德的高中老师约瑟夫·布里尔利到他海边的新家来看他。像往常一样，哈罗德有很多作品要写。哈罗德很高兴见到老师，也想让老师

was that he wanted him to read the play he'd just finished. Breaerley hadn't been there long, when Pinter asked his old teacher if he'd like to read his new play, "The Homecoming".

Brearley read the play and left without a word. He walked out the door and down to the beach. Pinter waited for him to return. When he came back, Brearley said he'd needed to quiet his feelings. He said the new play was wonderful, the best thing Pinter had ever written. Pinter was pleased. His teacher's opinion still meant a great deal to him—and with good reason. Brearley was right. When "The Homecoming" was performed, it was considered a turning point in Pinter's writing. He won a Tony Award[1] for the play in 1965, the year it opened. The play stunned[2] audiences with its depths of insight into the silent conflict between family members. One critic, John Lahr, said that with this play he became aware of words as "weapons of defense".

"The Homecoming" expresses the undercurrent[3] of tension between a husband and wife and between brothers and their father. Teddy brings his wife home to visit his family — his father and four

1. Tony Award: 托尼奖是戏剧界最知名的奖项之一，包括音乐剧。和电影界的奥斯卡奖颇为类似。美国剧联于 1946 年设立此奖，以著名女演员兼导演安朵涅特·佩里的名字命名 (Antoinette Perry Award)。
2. stun: v. 使晕倒，使眩晕，使震惊
3. undercurrent: n. 潜流，暗流

读他刚写完的剧本。布里尔利刚来一会儿，品特便向老师是否愿意读他的新作《归家》。

布里尔利读了剧本后，没说话就走了。他走出房门，走到海滩。品特等他回来。布里尔利回来后，说他当时要安静一下。他说新剧本太完美了，是品特最好的剧本。品特很高兴，老师的意见他还是很在乎——而且也确实值得在乎。布里尔利是对的，《归家》演出后，被认为是品特写作的转折点。1965 年《归家》上演，并为品特赢得了 1965 年托尼最佳剧本奖。这部戏探索了家庭成员之间沉默的冲突，其见识之深令观众倍感震惊。评论家约翰·拉尔说从《归家》开始，品特开始认识到语言是一种"防御武器"。

《归家》表达了夫妻、父子之间暗流涌动的紧张氛围。特迪第一次带

brothers — for the first time. The play ends with the disruption[1] of the family. Teddy goes back home, and his wife, Ruth, stays with his father and brothers.

Though this play doesn't necessarily reflect problems between Pinter and Vivien, his wife, they were still having trouble getting along together. At times, when the couple argued, Pinter wanted to leave the family, with all its demands. He thought about disappearing, just as his Uncle Judah had years ago.

Judah, his Mother's brother had been a boxer. Pinter was about ten years old when Judah just walked away from home and didn't come back. Harold saw his uncle only one other time in his whole life. It was almost a year later. Harold, his mother, and his grandmother were walking along the sidewalk. Judah rode by on the back of a garbage truck. They called out[2] to him. Judah made a sign to them, showing he recognized them, but he didn't ask the driver to stop. The truck went on down the street, with Harold, his mother, and his grandmother staring at their beloved relative as he rode away.

Instead of leaving home, Harold began an affair with another woman. His seven-year-affair with Joan Bakewell began in 1962 and continued until

1. disruption: *n.* 破坏，分裂，瓦解
2. call out: *v.* 呼喊，呼叫

妻子回老家，家里有父亲和四兄弟。该剧最终以家庭的分裂结束，特迪回了家，而他的妻子鲁思则同父亲和兄弟留在了一起。

该戏未必是品特和妻子维维恩之间问题的写照，不过他们相处得仍不顺利。有时吵起来，品特都想不顾一切，一走了之。他想过和舅舅朱达多年前一样突然失踪。

哈罗德的舅舅朱达曾是个拳击手。哈罗德十岁时，朱达离家出走，从此再没回来。哈罗德后来只见过舅舅一次。那是大约一年后，哈罗德和母亲、祖母走在路边，朱达坐在垃圾车后面路过。他们大声叫他，他仅打了个手势，表示认识他们，却没让司机停车。卡车驶离街道，哈罗德和母亲、祖母目睹着这位亲人的离去。

品特没有离家出走，而是和另一个女人开始了一段恋情。他和琼·贝克韦尔七年的恋情始于 1962 年，持续到 60 年代末。贝克韦尔爱过良好

almost the end of the decade. Bakewell was a well-educated, ambitious woman on the verge of a highly successful career. She became a well-known journalist. Three years younger than Pinter, she was liberal in many of her views and a free-thinker about sex.

She had a lot of company in her questions about the sanctity[1] of marriage. With many other young people, as well as a number of older people, in industrialized western countries during that period, she believed that sex between two consenting adults couldn't be, in itself, immoral. In the late 1960s and early 1970s, in England, France, and the United States in particular, philosophies of liberation, freedom, and self-expression were very popular. More people experimented sexually than ever before — in those countries, at least. Views about sexual freedom were linked to views about other individual liberties in general. Authority was questioned as never before. This opposition to authority may have been extreme in some ways, but it was warranted[2] in others. The questions grew out of recognition of the oppressive nature of some elements of government and industry. Young people spoke out against colonialism[3], against nuclear weapons, against the Vietnam War, and against racist and sexist laws. Other factors added to the spirit

1. sanctity: *n.* 圣洁
2. warranted: *adj.* 合理，能得到证明或支持
3. colonialism: *n.* 殖民主义

教育，充满抱负，正处在事业上升期，后成为知名记者。贝克韦尔比哈罗德小三岁，思想自由，性观念开放。

　　她对婚姻的圣洁性表示质疑，和她持同样观点的人不在少数。在那个工业化时期的欧洲，许多年轻人，以及一些年长者认为，成年人之间，只要你情我愿，发生性关系不算不道德。上世纪60年代末70年代初，在英国、法国，尤其是美国，解放、自由和自我表达的哲学大行其道。至少在英国、法国和美国，更多的人在性方面进行了尝试。人们把性自由的观点和其他有关个人自由的观点联系到了一起。权威受到前所未有的质疑。对权威的反抗在某些方面可能比较极端，但在其他方面却又有些合理。这些质疑有时是意识到了政府或企业的欺压本质。年轻人大声说出对殖民主义、核武器、越南战争以及具有种族或性别歧视意味的法律的反对。越来越多的女人摆脱家庭繁细，加入劳动大军。广告和电影对

of permissiveness[1]. More and more women were leaving the confines of home to join the workforce. The commercialization of sexuality in ads and on film especially made sex and romance glamorous. A small part was played by the availability of better forms of birth control, especially the birth control pill.

With Pinter's celebrity[2] came sexual temptation. Vivien had a lot of competition from the many smart, beautiful women interested in her famous husband. Their marriage couldn't withstand the pressure. However, Pinter's affair with Joan didn't bring their marriage to an end. Vivien and Harold stayed married for the time being[3]. They even moved to a new home together.

The two-hour drive from Worthing to London proved too much trouble for Pinter. His social and professional life was in London. In 1964, he bought a grand old house on Hanover Terrace in Regent Park in London. The house was built in 1820. It was designed by John Nash, the same architect who designed Caerhays Castle.

This huge six-story house didn't make their marriage better, however. Vivien must have worried that one reason Harold wanted to be in London

1. permissiveness: *n.* 放纵，纵容
2. celebrity: *n.* 名人，名声
3. for the time being: *adv.* 暂时

性进行商业化处理，给性和浪漫增添了美妙感。另外避孕措施发达，避孕药很容易买到，这也为性解放推波助澜。

品特的名气也带来了性的诱惑。维维恩面临着多年轻美貌的女子对丈夫的争夺。他们的婚姻承受不了这些压力。不过，品特和琼的恋爱并未终结他们的婚姻。维维恩和哈罗德暂时还维持着婚姻关系，他们甚至一起搬到了新家。

沃辛和伦敦之间两小时的车程对品特来说还是很麻烦。他的社交和职业生活都在伦敦。1964年，他在伦敦摄政王公园的汉诺威平地买了所大房子。房子建于1820年，由卡尔海斯城堡的设计者、建筑师约翰·纳什设计。

不过，六层楼高的大房子并未使他们的婚姻好转。维维恩担心，哈罗德来伦敦的原因之一，就是为了和其他女人有更多时间在一起。不过，

was to spend more time with other women. However, they still loved each other. Whatever their troubles, they enjoyed the solitude of the house. They didn't encourage people to drop in[1]. Pinter commented in one interview on the pleasure he got from just sitting together with Vivien in the kitchen, talking. They enjoyed each other's company.

Still, visitors to the house described it as silent. Such a large house had an insulating[2] effect on its occupants. In his book-lined study on the top floor, Harold wrote with hardly any interruption. From the windows he could see a lovely duck pond and a stretch of wooded park. His office had a bar, and he drank beer or Scotch during the day as he worked.

An interviewer who visited the Hanover Terrace home several years later said that on one wall of Pinter's study was a drawing by the modern artist, Picasso. On another wall was a balance sheet for his play "The Birthday Party". The balance sheet showed earnings of only 260 pounds in the short week the play ran at the Lyric Hammersmith Theater. If Pinter wanted to talk to someone on the lower floors of the house, and didn't want to leave his desk, he used the intercom. He and Vivien had luxurious surroundings, but the distance between them in their new house, seems poignant[3] in view of the future of their marriage.

1. drop in: v. 顺便走访，拜访
2. insulating: adj. 绝缘的，隔绝的
3. poignant: adj. 令人痛苦的，可悲的

他们仍然相爱。不管他们之间有什么问题，两人还是很享受与世相隔的生活。他们不鼓励别人来访。品特在一次采访中说到，他很喜欢和维维恩坐在厨房里说话。他们喜欢彼此相伴。

不过，去过那座房子的人都说它很安静。房子这么大，足以将居住者与外界隔绝。在顶层那间为书籍围绕的书房里，哈罗德可以不受打扰地勤奋写作。透过窗户，他可以看见宜人的鸭塘和一片带树林的公园。他的工作室里有个酒吧，平时，他可以边做事边喝啤酒或苏格兰威士忌。

几年后，一位访问过汉诺威平地的人说，品特书房的一面墙上挂着现代艺术家毕加索的画作，另一面墙上是《生日晚会》的资产负债表。资产负债表显示利里克·哈默史密斯剧院上演《生日晚会》不到一周内的收入只有260英镑。如果品特想和房子下面楼层的人说话，又不想离开书桌，就用内部通话机即可。他和维维恩有了奢侈的环境，但却在新屋里彼此拉开了距离。从他们后来的婚姻来看，这个距离显得很让人伤悲。

PLAYING ROLES

扮演角色

In the early 1960s, Pinter's works got more and more attention. In the spring of 1960, "A Night Out", and "The Birthday Party", were broadcast on television. In 1961 "The Collection" and "The Lover" were televised[1], with his wife Vivien playing the leading female role in both plays. Thousands of television viewers watched a kind of theater that two years earlier even many sophisticated[2] theater audiences found confusing. Television audiences might have preferred easier plays, but British television companies, especially the British Broadcasting Corporation, were dedicated to providing programs that were of higher quality than "sitcoms[3]" and musical variety shows[4]. Pinter's plays continued to be broadcast on BBC and other television stations with some frequency for the rest of his life. These television productions made his name even more familiar to the public than had his earlier radio and stage productions.

Of course, his plays continued to be performed on stage as well. In the early 1960s, his plays began to be performed in the United States, on the west coast and then on Broadway. The first professional production of one of his plays was "The Birthday Party". It was performed by the Actors' Workshop of San Francisco. American audiences were receptive[5] to his kind of playwriting — as least the more so-

1. televise: *v.* 通过电视播放
2. sophisticated: *adj.* 久经世故的，见多识广的，成熟的
3. sitcom: *n.* 情景喜剧
4. variety show: *n.* 杂耍
5. receptive: *adj.* 善于接受的，能接受的

1960 年代初期，品特的作品受到越来越多的关注。1960 年春，《外出一夜》和《生日晚会》通过电视播放。1961 年《集锦》和《情人》也搬上了电视荧屏，维维恩在两部剧中出演女主角。成千上万的观众通过电视，看到了这种两年前许多成熟的戏剧观众都感到困惑的戏剧。电视观众或许更喜欢简单的戏剧，但是英国电视公司，特别是 BBC，一直致力于提供高品位的节目，而不是情景喜剧和音乐杂耍。品特的戏剧后来一直在 BBC 和其他电视台播出。比起早期的广播剧和舞台剧，这些电视作品使品特更为大众熟知。

当然，品特的戏剧还一直在舞台上演出。上世纪 60 年代早期，他的戏剧也开始在美国演出，先是在西海岸，后来是百老汇。第一个专业制作的戏剧是《生日晚会》。它是由旧金山的演员工作室演出的。美国观众

phisticated theater-goers were.

During these years, Pinter didn't write any full-length plays[1], but he wrote many short sketches[2]. His sketch, "One to Another" opened at the Lyric Hammersmith Theater along with his "Trouble in the Works" and "Black and White". These short sketches continued the theme of struggle for dominance[3] between ordinary people, friends and relatives who both loved and despised each other.

In 1961, in Paris, Pinter met Samuel Beckett, the writer whom he most admired. Though it's not clear whether he was serious, Pinter claimed that the morning after the first night they met, Beckett went out at 5 AM to find some bicarbonate of soda[4]. He went to several different stores to find something to calm Pinter's stomach, which was upset from drinking too much the night before. Whether or not the story is true, the two writers became good friends. Beckett was one of the few writers whose influence Pinter acknowledged. Because of his competitive nature, Pinter seldom admitted any outside influences on his work.

An incident that happened about this time, but in the United States, shows both Pinter's competitive nature and how energetic he was. This incident

1. full-length play：n. 多幕剧
2. sketch：n. 短剧、小品
3. dominance：n. 统治，优势
4. bicarbonate of soda：小苏打

能够接受这种戏剧——至少成熟的戏剧观众能够接受。

那几年里，品特不写多幕剧，但写了很多短剧。他的短剧《相互》在利里克·哈默史密斯剧院与《风雨欲来》、《黑与白》一同上演。这些短剧继续以普通人——彼此之间既爱又恨的亲戚朋友——争取主导权为主题。

1961年，品特在巴黎见到了最为仰慕的作家塞缪尔·贝克特。尽管不清楚他的话是否属实，品特称他们头天晚上见面后，由于品特喝得太多，次日晨，贝克特五点便起床为他找小苏打水。他跑了好几家商店，想找这东西来给品特清肠胃。不管故事真实与否，两位作家成了朋友倒是真的。贝克特是少数几个品特坦承影响了他的作家之一。品特个性争强好胜，一般极少承认作品受到外在影响。

这期间在美国发生的一件事，说明了品特要强的个性和旺盛的精力。

happened in New Haven, Connecticut, during the first Broadway run of "The Caretaker". Sitting in a bar and more than a little drunk, an acquaintance challenged Pinter to a race one night. The two men, along with the other people they were with, left the bar. They walked outside and found a place to race. Someone signaled "go". Harold took off like an "electrified rabbit". The man who had challenged him to a race just stood there, amazed. He shrugged his shoulders and said he didn't really want to race after all. Everyone present knew that he was simply unwilling to race against such a strong runner. That Pinter took the man up on his challenge and that he ran with all his might shows something about his personality. Less competitive men might have let the challenge go unanswered. Less competent men might have lost the race.

In addition to appearing on radio, the stage, and television, Pinter's work soon began to appear on film. In December 1962, shooting for "The Caretaker", Pinter's first play to be filmed, began. The movie was filmed on location in Hackney, his childhood neighborhood in London's East End. After the movie premiered[1] in England, it opened under the title, "The Guest", in movie theaters in America. With his entry into film, Pinter's reputation[2] grew in international importance.

1. premier: *v.* 首映，首演
2. reputation: *n.* 名誉，名声

这事发生在康涅狄格州纽里文市，正值百老汇首次演出《看门人》期间。品特坐在酒吧里，喝得微微有些醉了，一个熟人向哈罗德发起短跑挑战。两人和其他人一道，离开了酒吧，到外头找了个地方，有人说"跑！"哈罗德就如"一只被电击中的兔子"一样跑将起来。向哈罗德发起挑战的人站在那里很是吃惊，他耸耸肩，说他其实不想比赛。在场的人都知道，他其实不想跟品特这样的劲敌赛。此事显示了品特的个性。遇到这种事，与世无争的人或许会不理睬这个挑战，能力平平的人或许会输掉比赛。

除了在广播、舞台和电视上出现，品特的作品不久开始出现在电影中。1962年12月，《看门人》成了品特第一部被改编为电影的剧本。电影在哈罗德童年住的伦敦东区哈克尼摄制，先在英国首映，后来以《来客》为名，在美国影院上映。进入电影圈后，哈罗德的国际知名度日渐上升。

During the early 1960s, Pinter also began to adapt other writers' novels for the screen. His first adaptation[1] was for the movie, "The Pumpkin-Eater". The movie was based on Penelope Mortimer's book about an unhappily married woman. This movie didn't get many good reviews. His second, better-known screenplay, "The Servant," based on a novel by Robin Maugham got a better reception. Like Pinter's original plays, both screenplays focus on the politics of personal relations. "The Servant" won two major awards: the British Screen-writers Guild Award for 1964 and the New York Film Critics Best Writing Award.

In adapting stories for movie scripts, Pinter learned to use tech-niques offered by the movie camera to handle fantasy and shifts in time. He felt freed from some of the conventions of the stage. Unlike William Faulkner, another famous author who wrote screenplays and disliked it very much, Harold Pinter enjoyed writing for the movies. He didn't regard writing scripts for movies as merely a means of making a living, as Faulkner did. Consequently, he was more suc-cessful at it.

During this time of his life, Pinter did a little acting, taking on roles in some productions of his

1. adaptation: *n.* 改编，改写

1960 年代初期，哈罗德开始将其他作家的小说改编为电影剧本。他的第一部改编剧本为《南瓜食客》。电影改编自佩内洛普·莫蒂默的小说，主人公是一个郁郁寡欢的已婚女子。这部改编电影反应平平。品特的第二部电影剧本《仆人》改编自罗宾·毛姆的小说，获得了较好反响。和他自己的剧作一样，品特的电影剧本关注错综复杂的人际关系。《仆人》赢得了两项大奖：1964 年英国剧作者协会奖和纽约影评人协会最佳剧本奖。

通过改编电影剧本，品特学会用电影摄影机处理幻想和时间挪移的技巧。他感到摆脱了舞台传统的某些束缚。另一位作家威廉·福克纳也曾写过电影剧本，但并不喜欢，仅作谋生手段。哈罗德·品特与其不同，他喜爱撰写电影剧本，在这方面也比福克纳更加成功。

在此期间，品特也曾演出，在自己的短剧中扮演了一些角色，他还

Chapter Twelve Playing Roles

own sketches. He also tried directing one of his plays. In June 1964, the Royal Shakespeare Company revived "The Birthday Party" in London. Pinter took on the job of directing the production. However, he found that he didn't like the results. He felt that at times the actors looked to him for the "right" way to enact their roles. He vowed that he would never direct any of his plays again.

With all that he had accomplished, in terms of his career, the most significant event for Pinter at this time was the production of his play, "The Homecoming". This play, which opened in London in June, 1965, was his last full-length play for many years. After it was written and produced, he seemed to have lost momentum[1].

Brearley had said it was his best play to date[2]. It was also his most controversial[3] play up to that time. The plot was shocking to many people. In a performance in New York City, some audience members left angrily during the second act. It is shocking to some audiences even today, not because of physical violence, but because of the sexual implications of the plot, which has a wife end her marriage and set up house-keeping with her husband's father and brothers. By the end of the play, it appears that she

1. momentum: *n.* 动力，势头
2. to date: *adv.* 至今，迄今
3. controversial: *adj.* 富有争议的

曾导演过自己的一部戏。1964 年 6 月，皇家莎士比亚公司在伦敦重演《生日晚会》，品特亲自执导，但觉得结果不尽如人意。他发现演员时不时来问他如何按"正确的"方式演绎角色。他发誓从此再也不导演自己的任何剧作了。

就事业上的成就而言，此时最大的事件是戏剧《归家》的上演。该戏于 1965 年 6 月在伦敦上演，此后，哈罗德在很多年里都没再写过多幕剧。在《归家》写完并上演后，品特似乎丧失了创作的动力。

布里尔利说《归家》是品特迄今为止最好的剧作，这亦是他最富争议的剧作。该戏的情节让很多人感到震惊。在纽约的一场演出中，有些观众在第二幕时愤而离场。时至今日，很多观众依然感到震惊，不是源于其中肢体冲突的暴力，而是因为情节里有性暗示，戏中妻子最后终结了婚姻，居然和丈夫的父兄留在一起做家务。该戏的尾声仿佛暗示她要

will have sex with the father and brothers and may also become a prostitute for one of the brothers, who is a pimp[1]. Pinter himself says that the characters in this drama do horrible things not because they're evil, but because they're desperate.

The play reminded one of Pinter's friends of an American playwright's work. Though Eugene O'Neill[2]'s plays are in a different style than Pinter's, two of them are famous for their dramatization of family tensions, including sexual tensions. O'Neill's "A Long Day's Journey into Night", and "Mourning Becomes Electra" dramatize intense underlying hostilities caused by power struggles within a family. Pinter's work isn't melodramatic[3], as O'Neill's work is. Pinter presents bizarre behavior, as though it were perfectly ordinary, but there is a similarity in theme. Pinter, however, firmly denied any influence of O'Neill's plays on his own.

"The Homecoming" is a troubling play. Pinter

1. pimp: *n.* 皮条客
2. Eugene O'Neill: 尤金·奥尼尔 (1888–1953)，美国戏剧的奠基人，生于纽约一个演员家庭，幼年随父亲的剧团走南闯北，漂泊无定。中学毕业后考入普林斯顿大学，后因酗酒闹事被开除学籍。在此后的冒险生活中，他曾到洪都拉斯淘过金，在非洲和南美当过水手，做过演员、导演、新闻记者、小职员等。1912 年患肺结核住院期间，他研读古希腊以来的戏剧经典作品，并开始戏剧创作，此后成为专业剧作家。奥尼尔是位多产作家，一生创作独幕剧21部，多幕剧28部。其中优秀剧作有：《东航卡迪夫》(*Bound East for Cardiff*, 1916)、《天边外》(*Beyond the Horizon*, 1920)、《琼斯皇》(*The Emperor Jones*, 1920)、《毛猿》(*The Hairy Ape*, 1922)、《榆树下的欲望》(*Desire Under the Elms*, 1924)、《大神布朗》(*The Great God Brown*, 1926)、《悲悼》(*Mourning Becomes Electra*, 1931)、《送冰人来了》(*The Iceman Cometh*, 1946)、《月照不幸人》(*A Moon for the Misbegotten*, 1957) 等。奥尼尔戏剧师承瑞典剧作家斯特林堡 (Strindberg) 和挪威剧作家易卜生 (Ibsen) 的艺术风格，把传统现实主义手法和现代表现主义技巧结合起来，挖掘人类心灵的底层。奥尼尔获得 1936 年诺贝尔文学奖。
3. melodramatic: *adj.* 具有情节剧特征的

和丈夫的父兄做爱，也可能会成为一名妓女，因为其中一个兄弟是个皮条客。品特说这部戏中的人物做恶事，并非因本性邪恶，而是因太过绝望。

该戏让品特的一位朋友想起了美国剧作家尤金·奥尼尔的剧作来。奥尼尔的戏剧风格与品特的风格迥异，但二者都善于表现家庭内的紧张关系，包括性关系方面的紧张。奥尼尔的《长日迷途入夜行》和《悲悼》将家庭内部的权力冲突所引发的潜藏敌意戏剧化了。品特的戏不像奥尼尔的那样注重情节。品特展现的是看似普遍的怪异举止，但却和奥尼尔呈现了同样的主题。但品特坚决否认受到过奥尼尔戏剧的影响。

《归家》是部令人不安的戏剧。品特的所有

based all his plays on his own experience. However, he argued with critics who thought the play was a "Jewish" play — though he did have the father of one of his Jewish friends in mind when he created the character of Max, the father in "The Homecoming". When Teddy, the husband, who is Jewish, brings his non-Jewish wife, Ruth, home to meet his father and brothers, conflict begins. But, while religion and religious views toward relations between men and women are important elements of the play, the drama can be interpreted in many different ways.

Some critics think of the play as having a feminist[1] viewpoint. They find a positive value in the wife's leaving a husband who doesn't see her as a whole person. Other critics find it hard to see Ruth's staying to take care of Teddy's father and brothers — perhaps sexually — as liberating.

To many critics, the play is another variation on Pinter's theme of power struggles between men when something desirable, usually a woman, is present. This theme has been interpreted in psychological terms, as well as in social ones. Critics use Freud[2]'s theories of psychology to claim that the play is basically a reflection of the universal wish of

1. feminist: *n.* 女权主义，女权主义者
2. Freud: 西格蒙德·弗洛伊德 (Sigmund Freud, 1856–1939)，奥地利医生兼心理学家、哲学家、精神分析学的创始人，著有《梦的解析》(*The Interpretation of Dreams*, 1900)

戏剧都基于自己的经历。不过，有些评论家认为这是部"犹太"戏剧，品特为之辩解。虽然他创作《归乡》中的父亲麦克斯这个人物时，心里确有一位朋友的犹太父亲作原型。当犹太丈夫特迪，带着非犹太妻子鲁思回家来见父兄时，冲突就开始了。即便宗教和宗教观对男女关系的影响是本剧的一大要素，该剧其实还可用许多不同的方式解读。

有些评论家认为该剧具有女权主义视角。他们发现，妻子离开不把她当做完人的丈夫，有着积极意义。可是鲁思留下来是伺候特迪父兄（或许是在性方面），所以也有一些评论家觉得"女性解放"一说实属牵强。

对许多评论家来说，这部戏也是品特作品中一个常见主题的演变：当某个理想物（通常是女人）出现时，男人之间会展开权力斗争。这个主题有心理学和社会学的解读。评论家根据弗洛伊德的心理学理论，认为该

all sons to get rid of their fathers and have their mothers all to themselves. In "The Homecoming", Teddy, the son, is also a father, in that he and Ruth have three sons. All of the men in the play compete for Ruth's favors.

So many of Pinter's plays are about triangles and about women's domination of men, that it's easy to argue that this psychological theme is important to his artistic imagination. A Freudian psychologist would propose that Pinter's plays repeatedly dramatize emotions he felt as a child. As an only son in a small family, he may have felt these emotions particularly intensely. He had no brother or sister to distract him from seeing who the real competitor for his mother's attention was. His father was his only competition. Moreover, his father was a hot-tempered man, a strict disciplinarian[1]. It's likely that, from early childhood, Pinter felt a more intense resentment toward him than many boys feel toward their fathers — which is not to say that he didn't love his father deeply.

In Pinter's plays, the dramatic action often takes place inside an apartment building or a house. Both houses and apartment buildings are, in psychologically symbolic terms, said to represent the mother. The ambivalence[2] that the men in Pinter's plays feel toward women is understandable in terms of the

> 1. disciplinarian: *n.* 厉行纪律的人
> 2. ambivalence: *n.* 矛盾，对立的情绪

戏基本上讲述了儿子摆脱父亲，独占母亲的愿望。在《归家》中，特迪既是儿子又是父亲，他和鲁恩生有三个儿子。戏中所有男人都想赢得鲁恩的好感。

品特很多戏的主题是三角恋和女性主导男性，很容易看出心理学主题在他艺术想象中的重要性。一位弗洛伊德心理学家认为品特的戏剧反复将其作为孩子时的感受戏剧化。作为小家庭中的独子，他的这种感受或许特别强烈。他没有兄弟姐妹来争夺母亲的关注，父亲是他唯一的竞争对象。而且他的父亲是个性格急躁、管教严格的人。有可能自童年时起，品特对他的憎恶就比其他男生对父亲的憎恶感都要强烈——当然，这不是说他心灵深处不爱父亲。

在品特的戏剧里，戏剧行动常发生在公寓或房间之内。房间和公寓，在心理学中象征着母亲。品特戏剧里男人对女人的矛盾心理，很类似于

ambivalence all children feel toward their mother, who represents what is unbearably dear. She is dear because she is the child's first and most important source of comfort, pleasure, and even life. Yet she can never belong fully and solely to the child. In Freudian theory, the child is jealous, but doesn't dare express jealousy against the powerful father figure.

Yet another critical approach to Pinter's plays sees them in terms of myth and ritual. In this view, the "king", or father, is overthrown as a sacrifice to the gods. His wife is then possessed by the new king — who will in turn be overthrown. Freud viewed such ritual as playing out the universal feelings he describes in his theories of the Oedipus complex, named for the Greek play in which Oedipus kills his father and marries his mother, without realizing who they are to him.

Though not all of Pinter's plays fit these critical patterns, most lend themselves to such interpretations and others as well. One of the attractions of his plays is that they can be studied through such various critical lenses.

儿童对母亲的矛盾心理。在孩子心目当中，母亲是不堪承受之亲。母亲很亲，因为她是孩子关怀、快乐甚至生命仰赖的最重要的来源，但是母亲永远无法完全专属于孩子。在弗洛伊德理论中，孩子嫉妒父亲，但是不敢向强大的父亲表达这种嫉妒。

也有人从神话和仪式的角度评论品特的剧作。按照这一视角，"王"或父亲，作为神的祭品被推翻。妻子被新王得到——而新王最终也会被推翻。弗洛伊德将这样的仪式看做是对一种普遍心理的释放，他称这种心理为"俄狄浦斯情结"。《俄狄浦斯》是一部希腊戏剧，剧中的俄狄浦斯王在一无所知的情况下弑父娶母。

不是品特所有的戏剧都可以这样去分析，但他大多数戏剧适合这些解读方式。品特戏剧的一大魅力，在于它们可用不同的批评方法加以阐释。

Chapter Thirteen

THE END OF A MARRIAGE

婚姻终结

During the late 1960s, the Pinters' careers were becoming more and more successful, even if their marriage wasn't. Pinter's plays on stage, on television, and in the movies continued to win him a wider audience and greater fame. His stage plays did the same for Vivien. In spite of their personal problems, she acted the lead female roles in many productions of his plays. She was also getting movie roles. In addition to playing Ruth in "The Homecoming" on stage, she played Ruth when the play was made into a movie. Her most famous role, however, was in the movie, "Alfie", in 1966. She was nominated for an Academy Award and a Golden Globe Award for Best Supporting Actress for her role in this movie. She won England's National Board of Review Award for the role.

They bloomed professionally in spite of the growing distance between them personally. Their marriage was increasingly stressful[1] to both of them. Pinter continued his affair with Joan Bakewell, meeting her almost every week in an apartment in one of London's seedier[2] neighborhoods. His life interfered[3] with his work to some extent. Though he undertook many writing projects, he suffered from writer's block[4] and didn't undertake the writing of any full-length plays. Instead, he worked on other things.

1. stressful: *adj.* 产生压力的，紧迫的
2. seedy: *adj.* 破烂的，破败的
3. interfere: *v.* 干扰，打扰
4. writer's block: *n.* 作家写作瓶颈，指作家才思枯竭的阶段

1960 年代末，品特一家事业春风得意，婚姻却每况愈下。品特的戏剧在舞台、电视、电影上演，他的观众越来越多，名气也越来越大。维维恩也是如此。尽管夫妻间存在问题，她仍在品特的许多剧中出演女主角，她还在电影中扮演角色。除了在《归家》的舞台剧中饰演鲁思外，她还在电影中扮演鲁思。维维恩最著名的角色，是在 1966 年的电影《阿尔菲》之中。她因此获得奥斯卡奖和金球奖最佳女配角提名，还获得了英国全国影评人协会奖。

二人的事业如日中天，关系却渐行渐远。婚姻对双方的压力越来越大。品特和琼·贝克韦尔的恋情仍在继续，他们每周都在伦敦一破落社区的公寓里见面。这样的生活影响了他的工作。他接受了许多写作任务，但开始遇到写作瓶颈，并不再写多幕剧，转而做其他事。

He continued writing movie scripts. He'd been commissioned[1] to write a screenplay adapting the novel, *The Berlin Memorandum*[2], by Adam Hall. In 1966, the movie, "The Quiller Memorandum", opened. This story about a spy was his first movie to be popular with a wide audience.

In June 1966, Pinter's contributions to literature and theater were so important that he was made a Commander of the Order of the British Empire[3]. This was a high honor. Only a few months later, he was honored in the United States, with a Tony award for his play, "The Homecoming", which had opened in Broadway in January, 1967.

With all of this going on in his life, it's understandable that during this period of life, he told a reporter that "Writing becomes more difficult the older you get."

"I'm thirty-seven years old now," Pinter said to the reporter. "And I feel as if I'm eighty years old."

About this time, an intersection[4] between Pinter's career and his marriage caused even more trouble between him and Vivien. He wrote "Landscape" while Vivien was playing in a production of "Macbeth". Two of his characters were Beth and Duff.

1. commission: *v.* 委托，委派
2. memorandum: *n.* 备忘录
3. Commander of the Order of the British Empire: 大英帝国司令勋章，是英国授勋及嘉奖制度中的一种骑士勋章，由英王乔治五世于1917年6月4日所创立，表彰给对英国社会贡献巨大的杰出人士，代表极高的荣誉
4. intersection: *n.* 十字路口

品特继续写电影剧本。他受托将亚当·霍尔的小说《柏林备忘录》改编成电影剧本。1966 年，电影《谍海群英会》上演，这部描述间谍的电影成为他第一部卖座的电影作品。

1966 年 6 月，品特因对文学和戏剧贡献巨大，获得了大英帝国司令勋章的殊荣。仅几个月后，他又在美国获得荣誉：1967 年 1 月在百老汇上演的《归家》获得托尼奖最佳戏剧奖。

荣誉纷至沓来。品特却对记者说"年龄越大，写作越难"。这个说法也在情理之中。

"我现在才 37 岁，"品特告诉记者，"可我觉得自己已经 80 岁了。"

就在此时，事业和婚姻的交错，使得品特和维维恩之间的问题更趋严重。此时他在写《风景》，而维维恩出演《麦克白》。他剧中的两个人

He took the names from the Shakespeare characters of Macbeth and Macduff. He gave the part of Beth to Peggy Ashcroft instead of to Vivien. Vivien was upset. It contributed to the end of his marriage.

In addition to being upset about strife[1] at home, Pinter was angry about the English government's censorship of his plays. In 1967, the government, through the office of the Lord Chamberlain[2], refused to allow performance of "Landscape". Pinter hated this censorship. He was resentful that one of his plays was to be kept off the stage because of one curse word in the play. This spat[3] with the government fueled Pinter's anger against any kind of censorship of art. He had long been opposed to authority that he thought overstepped its bounds, and he remained opposed for the rest of his life.

Stress results from any kind of excitement, whether good or bad. A year later, Pinter was pleased that another of his plays was filmed. The movie version of "The Birthday Party" opened in New York. However, this positive achievement cost him, too. It's no wonder that his affair with Bakewell was coming to an end. The life he was leading would have exhausted anyone.

1. strife: *n.* 冲突，竞争
2. Lord Chamberlain: *n.* (英国王室的) 公务大臣
3. spat: *n.* 口角

物叫贝丝 (Beth) 和达夫 (Duff)，取自莎士比亚的人物麦克白 (Macbeth) 和麦克达夫 (Macduff)。他将贝丝的角色给了佩姬·阿什克罗夫特，而没有给维维恩。维维恩很失望，这将他们的婚姻引向终结。

家庭争斗让品特失望，而他此时也对英国政府审查他的戏剧感到愤怒。1967 年，政府以公务大臣办公室的名义拒绝上演《风景》。品特讨厌审查制度，讨厌仅仅因为一个组咒的词语，整个戏剧竟无法搬上舞台。和政府的争吵增添了品特对任何艺术审查制度的愤怒。他一直反对政府的越界行为，后来也一直如此。

品特面临各种好坏刺激所带来的压力。一年以后，《生日晚会》电影版在纽约上映，品特很高兴。不过，这些积极的成就也是有代价的。也难怪他和贝克韦尔的恋情走向了终结。品特的生活，任何人卷入其中都会心力交瘁。

He had only brief liaisons[1] with women in the years from 1970 until he met the woman who would become his second wife — Antonia Fraser.

At the time Pinter met her, Antonia was married to Hugh Fraser, a Tory MP. They had been married for twenty-one years. They were the parents of six children — three daughters and three sons. Hugh Fraser was a Conservative member of the British Parliament. Antonia was a well-known author.

As the oldest of eight children of Earl and Lady Frank Pakenham, Antonia had been born into an aristocratic and intellectual family. She enjoyed a happy childhood in Oxford, where her father taught at Christ's Church. Like most little girls of her time, she liked playing with dolls, but she also showed the spirit of a tomboy[2]. Her parents recalled that one day when she was only three years old, she came into the house to tell them she'd killed a snake. When they went outside to look at what she'd done, they found a dead viper[3]. She'd killed it with the spade she was digging in the sand with.

Antonia also loved to read. She came from a family that knew the importance of learning and a

1. liaison: *n.* 联系，联络
2. tomboy: *n.* 行为似男孩子的女孩子，假小子
3. viper: *n.* 毒蛇

1970 年起他极少和女性有瓜葛，直到遇见后来成为他第二任妻子的女人——安东尼娅·弗雷泽。

品特见到安东尼娅时，她是保守党下院议员休·弗雷泽的妻子。他们结婚 21 年了，生了三男三女共六个孩子。休·弗雷泽是英国议会保守党议员，安东尼娅则是知名作家。

安东尼娅是弗兰克·帕克南伯爵夫妇的八个孩子中的老大，她生于贵族知识分子家庭。其父执教于牛津大学基督教堂学院，她在牛津度过了快乐的童年。和大多数小女孩一样，她喜欢玩偶，但也有假小子的脾气。据其父母回忆，她 3 岁时，有一天走进房子说刚杀了条蛇。父母走出房子，见到一条死了的毒蛇。她用沙铲杀死了毒蛇。

安东尼娅也喜爱阅读。她来自一个重视教育的家庭。父母把她送到

good education. They sent her to Dragon School at Oxford[1], where she was one of 40 girls and 400 boys attending at that time. Dragon School is a preparatory[2] school for children ages eight through thirteen. Antonia was happy there. She enjoyed her studies, and she liked playing rugby. After Dragon School, she went to a girls' boarding school and didn't like it at all. She changed from the girls' boarding school to attendance at a Catholic convent[3] school. She was happy again. She liked the convent school, partly because she found nuns interesting. When she was a teenager, she converted to Catholicism. Not long afterward, she came across a book of short biographies, *Eminent Victorians*, by Lytton Strachey. She loved the biographies and felt transported by them into a different world. She decided then and there what she wanted to do with her life — she wanted to write historical biographies.

She grew up to do just what she'd planned. She started her writing career with a children's book about King Arthur and the Knights of the Round Table. The next year she wrote a children's book about Robin Hood. After a book about dolls and a history of toys, she finally turned to biography.

1. Dragon School at Oxford: 飞龙中学，是英国牛津一所男女合校的寄宿制预备学校，始建于1877年，接收年龄在8到13岁之间的学生。该校教学质量优良，是英国最著名的预备学校之一。
2. preparatory: *adj.* 预备的
3. convent: *n.* 女修道院

牛津郡的飞龙中学，当时学校有400名男孩和40名女孩。飞龙中学是一所预备学校，招收年龄在8到13岁的孩子。安东尼娅在那里很开心，她喜欢学习，还喜欢打橄榄球。上了飞龙中学之后，她还上了所女子寄宿中学，但她不喜欢那学校。后来转入一所天主教女修道院学校，才又开心起来。她觉得修女很有趣，因而喜欢女修道院学校。十几岁时，她皈依了天主教。不久以后，她读到利顿·斯特雷奇的《维多利亚名人录》。她喜欢读名人传记，感觉阅读时仿佛进入了另一个世界。她那时就确立了自己的志向——写历史传记。

长大后，她果真实现了当初的设想。她职业生涯之初，写的是一本亚瑟王和圆桌骑士的儿童书，次年写了本关于罗宾汉的儿童读物，再后来写了本关于玩偶和玩具的历史书。最后，她转入了传记写作。

Fraser wrote biographies of several royal figures — Mary Queen of Scots, Queen Elizabeth I, Marie Antoinette, the wives of Henry the VIII, and others. Her biographies were praised for the quality of their scholarship as well as for their readability. Fraser also wrote several detective novels. They featured a fictional detective named Jemima Shore, who was clever and chic[1]. Because Fraser herself was clever and chic, she was invited to appear on television often to discuss her own and others' books.

Her husband's politics almost resulted in her being killed. In 1975, Antonia, her husband, and their friend, Caroline Kennedy — daughter of a former president of the United States, John F. Kennedy — just missed being blown up by an Irish Republican Army[2] (IRA) bomb. A neighbor, who was a well-known cancer researcher, happened to notice the device under the Fraser's car. The bomb went off as he got closer to look at it. The bomb killed this man instead of who it was intended for. As a Conservative Member of Parliament, Hugh Fraser was the intended target.

1. chic: *adj.* 高雅的
2. Irish Republican Army：爱尔兰共和军，成立于1919年，曾是爱尔兰新芬党的军事机构。总部设在都柏林，成员分布于南北爱尔兰，是由爱尔兰民族主义分子建立的一支反英的准军事游击队，目的是与驻爱尔兰的英军作战。2005年7月，爱尔兰共和军宣布，放弃武装斗争，加入和平进程。

弗雷泽为一些皇室成员写传记——苏格兰玛丽女王、伊丽莎白一世女王、玛丽·安托瓦内特、亨利八世的多位妻子，等等。她写的传记写作严谨，可读性强，备受读者赞誉。弗雷泽还写了几部侦探小说，以虚构的侦探杰迈玛·肖尔为主角。这位侦探机智而高雅。由于弗雷泽本人也十分机智而高雅，常受邀上电视讨论她和别人的作品。

安东尼娅丈夫的政治事业差点导致她被杀。1975年，安东尼娅和丈夫、他们的朋友卡洛琳·肯尼迪——美国前任总统约翰·肯尼迪的女儿——差点被爱尔兰共和军的炸弹炸死。他们的邻居——一位著名的癌症研究员——碰巧发现弗雷泽车底盘上装的炸弹装置。他走近汽车想看个究竟时，炸弹爆炸了，将他而不是弗雷泽炸死了。作为议会保守党议员的休·弗雷泽才是袭击目标。

Antonia Fraser met Harold Pinter first in 1971, but only briefly. They met a second time at a party four years later, in 1975. The two fell in love and began an affair. Pinter seems to have adored her from that moment until the end of his life. They lived together for two years before Fraser and her husband got a divorce.

In 1977, as his marriage with Vivien was dissolving, Pinter wrote a new drama, "Betrayal". This play draws on some details of his long affair with Joan Bakewell. On November 15, 1978, "Betrayal", opened in London at the National Theatre's Lyttleton Theatre. In January 1980, the Broadway premier of "Betrayal" opened. It was Pinter's first major commercial success in American theatre. The film of "Betrayal" was made in the house in West London in which Pinter and Bakewell had had an affair. If Vivien knew this to be the case, it no doubt hurt her deeply.

Not surprisingly, "Betrayal" portrays an emotional triangle. In this play, time is presented backward. The play dramatizes both professional and personal betrayal. Perhaps with his son in mind, Pinter shows how adult deceptions can affect the children within the web of these deceptions.

安东尼娅·弗雷泽1971年第一次见到哈罗德·品特，那次见面时间很短暂。四年后，他们在一次晚会上再次相见。两人相爱开始建立恋爱关系。从那时起直到逝世，品特都爱着她。在他们交往两年后，安东尼娅和丈夫离了婚。

1977年，就在品特和维维恩感情消逝之时，品特写了新剧《背叛》。这部戏透露了他和琼·贝克韦尔交往的某些细节。1978年11月15日，《背叛》在伦敦国家剧院的利特尔顿剧院演出。1980年1月，百老汇首演《背叛》，这是品特在美国戏剧界第一次获得商业上的成功。电影《背叛》在西伦敦的一所房子内拍摄，品特就是在那儿和贝克韦尔恋爱的。如果维维恩知道这些，一定会深受伤害。

顾名思义，《背叛》描绘的是一场三角恋。该戏用倒叙手法，将职业和个人的背叛搬上舞台。也许是写作时想到了儿子，品特还展示了成年人之间的欺骗将如何影响到孩子。

The high quality of this work is suggested by Samuel Beckett's sending Pinter a card praising "Betrayal". When Beckett died in 1989, the play was by his bedside. Pinter had managed to create art out of his imagination and the wreck of his marriage.

这部高质量的剧作得到了塞缪尔·贝克特的赞赏，他给品特寄了张贺卡，盛赞《背叛》。1989 年，贝克特逝世时，床边放着的就是这部戏。品特就是这样设法从想象和婚姻的残骸中创造出艺术。

Chapter Fourteen

THE BEGINNING OF A MARRIAGE

新的婚姻

When Pinter told his wife, Vivien that he loved Antonia and wanted a divorce, Vivien was furious[1]. In her upset, she made some hateful comments about Antonia to reporters. One of her remarks had to do with children. This was a sensitive[2] issue between her and Pinter. After the difficulties she had during Daniel's birth, she didn't want any more children. Harold, being an only child himself, had wanted Daniel to have a brother or sister. When Vivien talked to reporters, she focused on Antonia's having six sons and daughters.

"Antonia Fraser has charmed my husband. How she found time to do that, being the mother of six children, is hard for me to imagine," said Vivien.

Vivien told reporters that Pinter had left home without taking many of his clothes. "But," she added, "he can always wear her shoes — she has such big feet."

Vivien made these pitifully nasty remarks because she was angry. Jealousy clouded her judgment.

Antonia and her husband, Hugh Fraser, divorced because of the affair. Pinter moved in with Antonia in the home she had shared with Hugh in London's Kensington.

1. furious. *adj.* 狂怒的，狂躁的
2. sensitive. *adj.* 敏感的

品特告诉妻子维维恩他爱安东尼娅，想同她离婚。维维恩勃然大怒。盛怒之下，她向记者说了安东尼娅的坏话，其中有些与孩子有关。孩子是维维恩和品特之间的敏感话题。由于生丹尼尔时难产，维维恩不愿再生孩子。哈罗德作为独生子，本想让丹尼尔有个弟弟或妹妹。维维恩和记者交谈时，突出强调安东尼娅生了六个儿女。

"安东尼娅·弗雷泽勾引了我丈夫。作为六个孩子的母亲，她居然有时间来勾引人，真是匪夷所思，"维维恩说。

维维恩告诉记者说品特没带多少衣服就离开了家。"不过，"她补充道，"他可以穿她的鞋——她那双脚也够大的。"

出于愤怒，维维恩说出了这些可怜又刻薄的言论。醋意冲昏了她的头脑。

安东尼娅和丈夫休·弗雷泽因为这段婚外情已经离婚。品特搬出去和安东尼娅住，他们住在安东尼娅和休在伦敦肯辛顿的房子里。

In August, 1980, Pinter and Vivien were finally divorced — or so Pinter thought. In October, a couple of months later, Pinter and Antonia announced that they had gotten married secretly. In November, a month after their announcement, they learned that Vivien hadn't yet signed the divorce papers. This meant that Pinter and Antonia weren't legally married. As soon as Vivien signed the papers, Pinter and his new bride went through a second marriage ceremony. This time, the marriage was legal.

After her divorce from Pinter, Vivien never remarried. She began drinking heavily. She continued to drink for the rest of her life. Alcohol hurt this brilliant actress's career and eventually killed her. At fifty-three years of age, she died of liver disease.

Over the years, Vivien had been unable to recover from her upset about Pinter's leaving her. Her bitterness may have come partly from resentment at the advantages Antonia had in life. Vivien must have felt she hadn't a chance to win her husband back from someone of Antonia's caliber[1]. Both women were gifted and attractive, but Antonia had the confidence and poise that came from an excellent education. Her childhood as the daughter of an Oxford don[2] included meeting and talking with some of the best

1. caliber: *n.* 才干，品质
2. don: *n.* (英国牛津大学或剑桥大学的)指导老师，老师

1980 年 8 月，品特和维维恩终于离了婚——至少品特认为如此。两个月后，也就是 10 月，品特和安东尼娅宣布他们已经秘密结婚。11 月，在他们宣布结婚一个月后，他们得知维维恩还没在离婚文件上签字。这意味着品特和安东尼娅的婚姻没有法律效力。不过，维维恩一签字，品特和新娘就办了第二次婚礼，婚姻至此才生效。

和品特离婚后，维维恩一直未婚。她开始酗酒，直到逝世前一直如此。酒精毁了这位杰出女演员的事业，并最终害死了她。维维恩 53 岁时死于肝病。

很多年里，维维恩都没能从品特离开的失落中恢复过来。她的苦痛可能部分是因憎恨安东尼娅的优势而起。维维恩知道她无法从安东尼娅这种出色的女人那里把丈夫抢回来。这两个女人都很有才华和吸引力，但安东尼娅受过良好教育，语言出了自信和气质。作为牛津大学老师的女儿，安东尼娅童年时就同英国最优秀的思想家见面交谈。安东尼娅不

thinkers in England. Antonia not only grew up in Oxford's intellectual atmosphere, she went to college there. Vivien had never been to college. She was mostly self-educated. Antonia's family wasn't wealthy, but she had never known poverty. Vivien had gone through bad times when she and Harold were first married, with little money, living in a basement flat. Trying to care for the infant, Daniel, and earn money acting was exhausting. Sometimes Pinter brought the baby to the theater in the evening so Vivien could nurse him backstage. Once, the curtain had to be brought down for ten minutes because he was crying so loud. Vivien had to stop and feed him.

To some degree, too, Vivien's values alienated[1] her from her husband. She was — perhaps defensively — put off by what she saw as "heady[2]" talk about theater, literature, and other arts. She made her disdain of such discussions clear. On the other hand, Antonia, an author herself, dealt in ideas about history and the arts. Years earlier, Pinter had loved to talk about ideas with his friends in Hackney. Whatever other attractions she held for him, Antonia could enjoy sharing the banter[3] and challenges of that kind of companionship in a way that Vivien couldn't or wouldn't.

1. alienate: *v.* 疏远
2. heady: *adj.* 鲁莽的，冒失的
3. banter: *n.* 玩笑

仅生活在牛津大学的知识氛围里，还在那里上了大学。维维恩没上过大学，主要靠自学成才。安东尼娅的家庭虽不富裕，但却从没体验过贫穷的滋味。维维恩和哈罗德刚结婚时过过苦日子。那时他们钱不多，住在地下室。一边照顾儿子丹尼尔，一边演出挣钱很是辛苦。有时品特晚上把孩子带到剧院后台，好让维维恩在后台喂奶。有一次，丹尼尔哭声很大，幕布不得不降下十分钟，好让维维恩停下来给孩子喂奶。

某种程度上说，是维维恩的价值观导致她和丈夫疏远。或许出于自我保护，她厌恶关于剧院、文学和其他艺术的"冒失"谈话。她毫不掩饰对此类讨论的蔑视。与之相反，安东尼娅本身就是一位作家，热衷于历史和艺术之类的思想交流。许多年前，品特就喜欢和哈克尼的朋友交流思想。撇开其他魅力不谈，安东尼娅可以在这种深层次玩笑和挑战上游刃有余，这是维维恩做不到的。

The Pinters' son Daniel, though no longer a child at the time of his parents' divorce, also suffered after his father left home. Though he stayed for a short while with Pinter and Fraser, he stopped using the name Pinter. Instead, he took his grandmother's maiden name, Brand, for his last name. As Daniel Brand, he would become a musician. Not long after his parents divorced, Daniel left college because of a nervous breakdown[1]. Moving away from both parents, he went to live in Cambridgeshire, England.

The rift[2] in the Pinter family was never repaired. Two of Pinter's major plays, "The Homecoming" and "The Betrayal", drew on some of the problems in his first marriage. His efforts to forge a happy life within and outside this marriage brought a lot of emotional hardship on himself and on others. However cruel the behavior he, Antonia, and Vivien may have showed during the break up of his first marriage, Pinter's remark about the characters in "The Home-coming" applies to his situation in real life as well. His and Antonia's decision to divorce their spouses[3] and Vivien's angry public remarks to the press all came out of reasons that were "not evil, but slightly desperate".

1. nervous breakdown: *n.* (医学) 精神失常，崩溃
2. rift: *n.* 裂痕
3. spouses: *n.* 配偶

尽管品特夫妇的儿子丹尼尔此时已不再是小孩，也因父母的离婚而受伤害。他在品特和弗雷泽那儿住了一小段时间，但不再用品特这个姓，而改用祖母婚前的姓——布兰德——作为自己的姓。丹尼尔·布兰德后来成了音乐家。父母离婚后不久，丹尼尔因神经崩溃从大学退学，离开了父母，搬到英格兰剑桥郡住。

品特家庭的裂痕永远无法弥补。品特的两部主要戏剧，《归家》和《背叛》，都用第一次婚姻中的问题做素材。品特在婚里婚外为了幸福生活做的努力给自己和他人带来了情感压力。不论他、安东尼娅和维维恩在品特第一次婚姻破裂时的做法如何无情，品特在《归家》里对人物的评论也同样适用于现实生活中的他自己。他和安东尼娅离开各自配偶的决定，以及维维恩公开向媒体发表的愤怒言论，都"不是出于恶意，而是有些绝望"。

1. *The French Lieutenant's Woman*: 《法国中尉的女人》(1969)，约翰·福尔斯一部实验性很强的小说，故事发生在1867年的英国。查尔斯在小镇莱姆会见未婚妻蒂娜，在海边，他遇见被人们称为"法国中尉的女人"的萨拉，并为她神秘的诱惑力吸引。随着他们关系日益密切，福尔斯在此为小说安排了三种不同的结局。《法国中尉的女人》的主题是自由，福尔斯采用开放性结局，放弃对人物和情节的绝对控制权，邀请读者参与创作，三种结局使小说含有偶然与必然、选择与命运等一系列哲学意味。

2. John Fowles: 约翰·福尔斯(1926－2005)，英国小说家，主要作品有《收藏家》(*The Collector*, 1963)、《大法师》(*The Magus*, 1965)、《法国中尉的女人》、《埃伯尼塔楼》(*The Ebony Tower*, 1974)等。

After he married a second time, he kept writing. Some critics said that he never again achieved the greatness found in some of his earlier plays. Whether or not that is true, he wrote no new full-length plays until "Moonlight", years later, in 1994. Long before that time, the furor over his second marriage had ended.

He spent much of his time over the next twenty-five years writing screenplays based on other authors' stories. One of the most famous movies he wrote screenplays for is *The French Lieutenant's Woman*[1]. Released in 1981, it took him over a year to write. It is thought to be the best screenplay he ever wrote. Interestingly, this film is about an unhappy marriage. John Fowles[2], author of the novel, provides two endings to his readers. One ending to this

第二次结婚后，品特坚持写作。有些评论家认为他再未达到一些早期作品的高度。这种说法正确与否姑且不谈，多年后，直到1994年，他才又写了一部多幕剧《月光》。早在那之前，第二次婚姻的激情已经逝去。

接下来20年的时间里，品特将其他作家的原著改编成电影剧本。其中，最著名的电影就是《法国中尉的女人》。电影1981年上映，改编剧本花了他一年时间，那是他写过的最好的电影剧本。有趣的是，这部电影讲的也是不幸的婚姻。小说作者约翰·福尔斯为读者提供了两种结局。一个结局是以代表19世纪英国传统的维多利亚时代为背景：丈夫接受了不愉快的婚姻，并维持着局面。第二个结局是丈夫

story — which is set in Victorian times[1] — represents nineteenth-century English tradition. The husband accepts his unhappy marriage and stays with it. In the second ending, the husband leaves his wife. He asks the woman he's fallen in love with to marry him, but she says no. For the screenplay, Pinter invents a new frame to accommodate[2] Fowles' use of a twentieth-century viewpoint to tell a story set in Victorian England. Pinter has the leading characters play dual roles. They play twentieth-century actors making a film set in Victorian times. For the screenplay, Pinter also invents a third ending, a happy, if vague, one. In the film, the line between illusion and reality becomes blurred[3], as does the line between present and past.

In 1982, the following year, Pinter's stage play, "Betrayal", was made into a movie. The movie follows closely the action of the stage play, which Pinter wrote after he was living with Antonia. As with the stage play, the movie plays a trick with time. The audience sees the end of the affair first and progresses backward in time to the lovers' first meeting, which comes at the end of the movie. Watching the lovers' past from the vantage of the future makes their

1. Victorian times : n. 维多利亚时代，指1837－1901年，即英国维多利亚女王 (Queen Victoria) 在位的63年，是英国最强盛的所谓 "日不落帝国" 时期，在此期间，英国在工业、经济、文化等方面都处于巅峰
2. accommodate : v. 提供，适应
3. blur : v. (视线，界限的) 模糊不清

离开了妻子，他要所爱的女人嫁给他，但遭到拒绝。创作电影剧本时，品特发明了一种新的框架来适应福尔斯用20世纪视角讲述的维多利亚时期的英国故事。品特让主角扮演双重角色，他们以20世纪演员的身份来演维多利亚时代的电影。同时，品特为电影剧本发明了第三种结局，一个快乐而稍显模糊的结局。在电影里，幻想和现实、现在和过去的界限变得模糊不清。

1982年，品特的舞台剧《背叛》拍成了电影。电影严格按照舞台动作，品特是在和安东尼娅住一起时写的《背叛》。一如舞台剧，电影有些时间安排上的炫技。观众首先看见故事结尾，然后由过程逐步倒退到恋人的初次聚会，至此剧终。在知道恋人结局的情况下看到恋人的过去

doomed affair poignant. Knowing that the lovers ultimately decide to end their affair also gives an ironic turn to many of the things the lovers do and say.

When he fell in love with Antonia, Pinter had already been through a seven-year affair with Joan Bakewell. He dramatized this affair through an artistic effort that framed it in painful terms. After all, the two characters in "Betrayal" deciding to end their affair may have been the ultimate betrayal in the play. In an important sense, having betrayed their spouses in starting the affair, the two lovers betray themselves in giving it up. Neither of them feels love toward *anyone* — friend, spouse, or lover — deeply enough to be loyal. Pinter had good reason not to repeat this last betrayal in his love affair with Antonia, regardless of how others felt about his leaving his family. There were no painless choices available to him.

In 1982, when Vivien died, Pinter was devastated. She'd been his wife for eighteen years of marriage. Besides, her death signaled the end of his youth. He was fifty-two years old. Antonia's children's children called him "granddaddy". Pinter was still energetic and strong, but the end of his life seemed suddenly more real.

那注定失败的结局更令人痛苦。知道恋人最终要分开，恋人眼前的所作所为显得极具讽刺意味。

和安东尼娅相恋的时候，品特就已经结束了和贝克韦尔长达七年的恋情。他将这段恋情通过艺术手段加以戏剧化，使之变得悲伤。毕竟，《背叛》中的两个人物决定结束恋情或许是剧中最根本的背叛。他们开始恋情就已经背叛了配偶，两位恋人放弃恋情也是背叛自己。他们两人对任何人——朋友、配偶或是情人——都没有深到能让其产生忠诚的爱。不管别人怎么看他抛弃家庭，品特有理由在和安东尼娅的恋情里不再重蹈覆辙。对他来说，没有痛苦的选择对他来说并不存在。

1982 年，维维恩逝世，品特悲痛欲绝。维维恩和品特毕竟携手走过了 18 年。维维恩的死也标志着品特青春的终结。他已经 52 岁了，安东尼娅的孙子辈都叫他"爷爷"。品特虽然仍强健有力，但死亡突然变得更加真实。

Chapter Fifteen

POLITICAL DRAMA

政治戏剧

The late 1960s and early 1970s were times of political unrest. In the United States and in France the unrest was closely related to the Vietnam War. In England, unrest was more cultural than political. London was referred to in the popular press as "swinging[1]" because of the new sexual freedom there, the international fame of The Beatles[2] and other music groups, and a youthful fashion industry. During these decades, Pinter's politics were mostly in evidence indirectly. Though he'd never been a fan of government, he became much more vocal and active in opposing particular government actions in the 1980s and 1990s. He joined political organizations and spoke out against government oppression.

In a way, he was more social during this time. In commenting on his marriage to Vivien at one point after their divorce, he said that she was a "pretty solitary person".

"She has no women friends," he added.

These remarks suggest a contrast with Antonia, who had many friends. His second wife may have encouraged Pinter's greater participation in social and political realms. Antonia's parents were highly political. Her mother had been a socialist in the

1. swinging: *adj.* 多姿多彩的
2. The Beatles: 披头士乐队，又译甲壳虫乐队，是英国流行音乐史上最伟大、最有影响力、拥有最多歌迷、最为成功的乐队

20世纪60年代末70年代初是政局动荡的时代。美国和法国出现的政局动荡和越南战争有关。而在英国，动荡的文化成分多过政治成分。伦敦被大众媒体称作"色彩纷呈"之都。这里性自由方兴未艾，有披头士乐队等享有国际盛誉的乐队，还有朝气蓬勃的服装业。这些年间，品特的政治观点并非直接表露。品特从来不喜欢政府，在八九十年代，他以越来越多的言辞和行动抨击政府的某些举措。他参加政治组织，公开反对政府的压迫。

在此期间，他社交活动频繁。在评价他和维维恩的婚姻时，他说维维恩是个"美丽而孤独的人"。

"她没有女性朋友，"他补充说。

这话说明维维恩和朋友众多的安东尼娅对比鲜明。品特的第二任妻子可能曾鼓励他更多地投身政治和社会活动。安东尼娅的父母积极参与

1930s and had run, unsuccessfully, as a Labour Party candidate for office. Antonia's father was also a member of the Labour Party. He advocated strongly for rehabilitation of criminals[1] and against pornography[2]. Antonia shared many of her parents' political views, as well as their religious beliefs.

That there was some change in Pinter's political views is shown by his statements about Prime Minister, Margaret Thatcher[3], a Conservative. In 1979, he'd voted for Thatcher. By the early 1980s, he said he'd been an idiot to vote for her.

In 1985, as a vice-president of the English branch of PEN[4], Pinter and the American playwright, Arthur Miller, who was vice-president of the American branch, flew to Turkey. They went to express solidarity with dissident[5] writers there. Some of the writers had been imprisoned. Pinter and Miller talked to many writers there. Some of them said they'd undergone torture while in prison. The two playwrights presented a petition[6] signed by over two thousand writers, scientists, and clergy-

1. rehabilitation of criminals：帮助罪犯重返社会的援助行动
2. pornography：*n.* 色情文学，色情描写
3. Margaret Thatcher：玛格丽特·撒切尔 (Margaret Hilda Thatcher, 1925–)，政治家，1979 至 1990 年任英国首相，1975 至 1990 年任保守党领袖，在任期间成就卓著，被誉为"铁娘子"
4. PEN：*abbr.* International Association of Poets, Playwrights, Editors, Essayists, and Novelists 国际笔会
5. dissident：*n.* 持不同政见者，异见分子
6. petition：*n.* 请愿，请愿书

政治：她的母亲 30 年代曾是社会党党员，还曾作为工党候选人参加竞选，但最后落选。安东尼娅的父亲也是工党党员，他强烈支持罪犯重返社会的辅导项目，反对色情。安东尼娅和父母的政治观点和宗教信仰一致。

品特的政治观点前后也发生了变化，这表现在他对保守党英国首相玛格丽特·撒切尔的言论上。1979 年他投票给了撒切尔。而到了 80 年代初，他说投票支持撒切尔实属白痴之举。

1985 年，品特作为国际笔会英国分会副主席，和美国剧作家、国际笔会美国分会副主席阿瑟·米勒一起飞赴土耳其。一些土耳其作家遭到关押，他们去表示对土耳其异见作家的支持。品特和米勒同许多土耳其作家交谈。有些作家说他们在监狱中受过拷打。两位剧作家递交了一份由两千多位作家、科学家和神职人员签名的反对虐待异见分子的请愿书。

men protesting this treatment of dissidents. Pinter and Miller held a joint news conference in Istanbul calling attention to the issue.

During their visit to Turkey, the two playwrights attended a party at the U.S. Embassy in Ankara. Arthur Miller was the guest of honor[1]. At the party, both Pinter and Miller made clear their opposition to the Turkish government's treatment of prisoners. They also questioned U.S. support for the Turkish dictatorship. Miller remained mild-mannered and polite. Pinter argued over dinner with a Turkish woman. He insulted the U.S. ambassador in a conversation with him after dinner.

"I remind you, sir, that you're a guest in my home," the Ambassador said coldly and turned his back on Pinter.

Pinter took that as an invitation to leave the party. Miller left the embassy with Pinter.

Pinter and Miller were not in any serious danger during their visit to Turkey; however, they heard that the Turkish government put out an order to arrest them. Their visit drew more international attention to the mistreatment of political prisoners there.

Though the press has at times disparaged[2] his political efforts as "champagne socialism", Pinter's

1. guest of honor: *n.* 主宾，贵宾
2. disparage: *v.* 蔑视，贬低

品特和米勒在伊斯坦布尔召开联合记者招待会，呼吁人们关注此事。

访问土耳其期间，两位剧作家出席了驻安卡拉美国大使馆举办的晚宴。阿瑟·米勒是贵宾。宴会上，品特和米勒都明确表示反对土耳其政府虐待犯人。他们还对美国政府支持土耳其专治政府的做法提出了质疑。米勒态度始终温和礼貌，哈罗德则和一位土耳其的女争了起来。晚宴后，品特和美国大使谈话，又将他侮辱了一番。

"我提醒您，先生，您是我这里的客人，"大使冷冷地说，转身不理品特了。

品特把这句话当做逐客令，米勒和品特一起离开了大使馆。

品特和米勒在土耳其访问期间危险不大，但他们听说土耳其政府要逮捕他们。他们的访问吸引了国际社会对土耳其政府虐待政治犯的关注。

媒体有时把品特的政治努力贬称为"香槟酒社会主义"，但品特的活

activities were often productive, at least in making representatives of the English government uncomfortable in some of their actions.

During the late 1980s, Pinter wrote some of his most famous screenplays. Some of these had political themes. His screenplay for *Reunion*, based on a novella[1] by Fred Uhlman, took him back to the war of his childhood days. Pinter's mother had recommended that he read Uhlman's book, about a friendship between two German boys, one of them Jewish. The tale begins after World War II, but flashes back to it. It is a story of sacrifice and loyalty. Pinter worked on this screenplay for three years, between 1987 and 1990.

Whether the movie, *The Trial*[2], for which Pinter wrote the screenplay, is political or not, is debatable. Pinter says it is not. He sees the story as questioning the unexplainable behavior of an all-powerful God. The film's director, however, talks about the movie differently. He emphasizes Pinter's affinity[3] with Kafka[4] as inspired by their shared Jewish background. Pinter had long admired Kafka's work and was happy to write the screenplay. His parents must have been proud of his work on this film, as well as his work

1. novella: *n.* 中篇小说
2. *The Trial*: 《审判》(*Der Prozess*, 1925) 是卡夫卡写的一部长篇小说。小说的主人公约瑟夫·K在一个早上被唤醒后,不明原因地被捕,陷入一场难缠的官司之中,却不知道自己的罪名。K最终在一个黑夜里被带走,并秘密处死
3. affinity: *n.* 亲密关系,吸引力
4. Kafka: 弗朗茨·卡夫卡 (Franz Kafka, 1883–1924), 德国小说家。卡夫卡文笔明净而想像奇诡,常采用寓言体,背后的寓意言人人殊,见仁见智。主要作品有《变形记》(*Die Verwandlung*, 1915)、《审判》(*Der Prozeß*, 1925)、《城堡》(*Das Schloß*, 1926) 等

动常常卓有成效,至少全让英国政府的人员感到很尴尬。

80年代末,品特写了几部著名的电影剧本。有些剧本含有政治主题。电影剧本《回归》改编自佛瑞德·乌尔曼的中篇小说。这部剧本把他带回童年时期的战争。品特的母亲建议他读一读乌尔曼这本关于两个德国小男孩之间的友谊的书,书中的一个男孩是犹太人。故事始于二战后,通过倒叙手法讲述,这是部关于奉献和忠诚的小说。从1987年到1990年,品特花了三年时间将其改编成剧本。

品特改写的《审判》是不是部政治电影尚有待商榷。品特说《审判》不是政治电影,他将其看做对全能上帝费解行为的质询。而电影导演的看法却不同,他强调品特和卡夫卡的相似性,认为二人都受到犹太背景影响。品特一直崇拜卡夫卡的作品,因此乐意改编剧本。品特的父母肯定为

on *Reunion*.

Much as they loved their famous son, they still found themselves in conflict with him over issues related to Judaism. Pinter's father was a Zionist[1]. He fully believed in Israel's moral right to occupy what had been Palestinian land in the Middle East. Pinter opposed many of Israel's actions toward the Palestinian refugees. They had loud arguments when they clashed over Israeli political and military action.

Both Pinter and his father were emotional men. Pinter's anger was famous, if exaggerated, in the press. Some of his lifelong hatred of oppression and cruelty came out of boyhood conflicts with his some-times overbearing father.

Pinter's original dramas written during this period also reflect his interest in public politics and his long hatred of domination of one person over another. His short play, "Mountain Language", dedicated to Antonia Fraser, was first performed in 1988. Pinter himself directed it at the National Theatre in London. This was not the first play that he had directed since his early bad experience with directing "The Birthday Party". It was, however, one of the most original of his later plays, regardless of who directed it.

1. Zionist *n.* 支持或拥护犹太复国运动者

他改编《审判》和《回归》而感到骄傲。

品特的父母深爱自己出名的儿子，但他们仍然发现和品特在犹太教问题上意见相左。品特的父亲是犹太复国主义者，他完全相信以色列占领中东巴勒斯坦领土的道德正义性。品特则反对以色列对待巴勒斯坦难民的许多行动。他们常就以色列的政治和军事行动争吵。

品特和父亲都是情绪化的人。品特易怒的脾气，一经媒体的夸张报道，变得人所皆知。品特毕生憎恨镇压和残暴，这种心态，部分是因童年时期他的父亲有时候显得比较霸道，他和父亲之间关系紧张。

在此期间，品特的戏剧还反映了他对公共政治的兴趣，以及他对人压迫人的憎恶。他献给安东尼娅·弗雷泽的短剧《山地语言》于1988年首演。品特亲自执导这部戏剧，后来在伦敦的国家剧院上演。这并不是《生日晚会》失败以来他所导演的第一部戏剧。不过，不论谁做导演，该剧都是品特晚期最富原创性的作品之一。

"Mountain Language" is a twenty-minute montage[1], a series of images on the theme of language and oppression. In this play, the mountain people are forbidden to speak their language. They're only allowed to speak the language of the capital. They're told their language is forbidden because it is "dead". Full of curse words, the play shows the futility and barrenness of language when put to some purposes. Though the play never names the country, Pinter wrote it after being in Turkey and talking with Kurdish[2] dissidents. However, the dialogue is full of English slang[3]. The only names used in the play are English names. In not naming the government or country, he implies that the cruelties it shows are going on in many places in the world. One of the interesting things about the play, too, is that it criticizes itself. The dialogue makes clear that, as a play, it in some ways goes along and even makes use of the abuse of power. "Mountain Language" is a complex, if fragmentary[4], drama. In it, Pinter uses new methods to extend his dramatization of struggles for power between family and friends into the political realm.

In the autumn of 1989, the playwright traveled to New York to work with the Classic Stage

1. montage: *n.* 蒙太奇，文学音乐或美术的组合体的音译，原为建筑学术语，意为构成、装配，现在是影视电影创作的主要叙述手段和表现手段之一，一般包括画面剪辑和画面合成两方面，画面剪辑（由许多画面或图样并列或叠化而成的一个统一图画作品），画面合成（制作这种组合方式的艺术或过程）

2. Kurdish: *adj.* 库尔德人，库尔德人的

3. slang: *n.* 俚语，行话

4. fragmentary: *adj.* 碎片化的，碎片的

《山地语言》是一部长达20分钟的蒙太奇式作品，是一系列关于语言和压迫的图像叠加。剧中山地人不准说自己的方言，只准用首都的语言说话。他们被禁止说山地语言，因为山地语言已经"消亡"。全剧充满咒骂，展示了语言若是用于某些目的，会落入无益、贫瘠的境地。剧中没有点名，但该剧是品特访问土耳其并和库尔德异见分子谈话后写的。不过，台词中英国俚语比比皆是，剧中出现的人名也是英语人名。不点出政府和国家的名字，品特是要暗示这样残忍的行径，在世界上许多地方发生着。剧中一个有趣的现象是，戏剧也做自我批评。剧中台词也表现出权力的滥用，甚至有时是在刻意滥用。《山地语言》或许有些支离破碎，但它是部复杂的戏剧。剧中品特运用新方法，将原本局限于家人朋友之间的权力斗争，扩展至政治领域，并将其戏剧化了。

1989年秋天，品特飞到纽约和经典舞台剧团公司一起工作。剧团想

Company Repertory. The CSC wanted to produce a "double-bill[1]" performance of two of his plays. This performance would combine productions of "Mountain Language" and "The Birthday Party". Their production would be the American premier of "Mountain Language". Pinter's friend, actress, Lauren Bacall, had told him about CSC's powerful revival of "The Birthday Party" the year before. In support of their work, he offered CSC the exclusive American rights to "Mountain Language". More, he agreed to help them plan and rehearse the production. The CSC artistic director, Carey Perloff, was impressed with Pinter's commitment to their production. She and the actors involved in this production found his help invaluable. In her written description of this experience, she praises him for the generous, intelligent, and practical advice he offered during their preparations for performing these two plays.

This commitment was made and carried out during a period in Pinter's life when his time was divided between many causes. He belonged to the Cuba Solidarity campaign to end the United States blockade of that country. He belonged to an international committee to defend Serbian[2] dictator Slobodan Milosevic.

1. double-bill: *n.* 两场戏剧合演的
2. Serbian: *adj.* 塞尔维亚人，塞尔维亚语的

同时上演品特的两部戏剧：《山地语言》和《生日晚会》。此次演出是《山地语言》在美国的首演。品特的朋友、女演员劳伦·白考尔告诉品特经典舞台剧团去年对《生日晚会》的成功重演。作为对演出的支持，品特授权经典舞台剧团在美国独家演出《山地语言》。他还答应帮助他们排练戏剧。剧团艺术指导凯莉·珀洛夫对品特的尽心尽力印象深刻，她和演员都认为品特给了很大帮助。在笔记中，她赞赏品特在两场戏排演中提出的慷慨、明智、实用的建议。

帮助该美国剧团的同时，品特百务缠身。他是古巴团结运动的一员，该运动旨在结束美国对古巴的封锁；他还属于一个为塞尔维亚独裁者斯

He participated in public protests outside the American Embassy in London because of United States' actions in Nicaragua. He and thousands of others protested the sending of a military force, the "contras", to overturn[1] the new socialist government there.

Pinter's political commitments brought him many enemies. He was criticized as too vulgar and accused of being involved politically just to get publicity for his writing. However, his new commitments also made him many friends. His major biographer, Michael Billington, quotes a Latin American writer's birthday tribute[2] to Pinter. The Latin American author compares Pinter's artistic vision with that of his compatriots, saying that these visions support each other in their differences. The author ends his tribute by saying, "Pinter is truly ours, in Mexico, Nicaragua or Argentina."

Pinter's political commitments of the 1980s and 1990s carried over[3] into a new century. One of his most outspoken oppositions was against the United States' invasion of Iraq in 2003. He spoke on many public occasions against the aggression to bring a change in regime there. He spoke out against England's

1. overturn: *v.* 推翻，颠覆
2. tribute: *n.* 颂词
3. carry over: *v.* 继续，延期至

洛博丹·米洛舍维奇辩护的国际委员会；他参加了美国驻伦敦大使馆外就美国在尼加拉瓜行动的公开抗议。他和成千上万其他人抗议美国派遣军队，或曰"反政府军"，颠覆新成立的社会主义政权。

品特的政治活动也让他树敌无数。人们批评他太粗俗，也有人批评他参与政治只是为了让自己的作品得到公众注意。不过，他的政治兴趣也为他赢得了许多朋友。他的主要传记作者米歇尔·比林顿引述了一位拉美作家致品特的生日颂词。这位拉美作家将品特的艺术视野和他的同胞相比，他说尽管存在分歧，但正是这些视野使他们互相支持。这位作家在颂词最后写道，"品特真正属于我们，属于墨西哥，属于尼加拉瓜，属于阿根廷。"

品特在八九十年代的政治兴趣进入新世纪后仍在延续。他毫无顾忌地反对美国2003年入侵伊拉克。他在许多公共场合发表声明反对入侵伊拉克以推翻伊拉克政权。他也抨击英国对伊战的支持——他加入到以战

support for the Iraq war, too — joining the movement to prosecute[1] England's Prime Minister, Tony Blair, for war crimes.

The young man who had refused to serve in England's army years ago was growing old, but he hadn't given up the struggle to find meaning in life. He enjoyed the fight.

1. prosecute v. 起诉，告发

争罪起诉英国首相托尼·布莱尔的联合运动中。

这位多年前拒绝在英军服役的年轻人虽然垂垂老矣，但是他从未放弃追寻生命意义的斗争。他热爱战斗。

Chapter Sixteen

IN SICKNESS AND IN HEALTH

疾病与健康

Not long after the turn of the century, Pinter faced a new fight. He was diagnosed with cancer of the esophagus[1] in December, 2002. Esophageal cancer affects the canal between the mouth and stomach. Difficulty in swallowing, weight loss, and feeling tired are among the most common symptoms[2]. Because this cancer is usually discovered late in the course of its disease, the quality of life of its sufferers is often poor. The survival rate is low. Only about eight percent of those diagnosed with esophageal cancer survive it. The cause of the cancer isn't known. Some research links it to smoking. In his younger days, Pinter was a heavy smoker. However, there isn't a clear causal link between his smoking and his cancer. Heavy drinking is also associated with esophageal cancer. Pinter drank regularly, but not so heavily. The disease appears more frequently in men than in women. Whether this is due to genetic differences or lifestyle differences isn't certain. Like most cancers, esophageal cancer tends to appear in older people.

Soon after the diagnosis, Pinter went into the Royal Marsden Hospital in London for surgery. The operation to remove the cancer cells in his throat was a success. He credited his surgeon with being brilliant, but he gave his wife credit too.

1. esophagus: *n.* 食道
2. symptom: *n.* 症状，征兆

新世纪之初，品特又面临一场新的战斗。2002年12月，他被诊断出食道癌。食道癌损害口腔和胃之间的喉管，最常见的症状是吞咽困难，体重减轻，身体疲惫。食道癌通常到晚期才能发现，患者的生活质量通常会下降。食道癌存活率很低，大约不到8%。食道癌的起因尚不清楚，一些研究人员认为是抽烟引发的。品特年轻时抽烟很多，但没有明确的证据表明是抽烟引发食道癌。过量饮酒也会引发食道癌。品特常饮酒，但并不是时常过量。食道癌患者男性多过女性，究竟是由基因引起的，还是生活方式引起的，尚不明确。和大多癌症一样，食道癌患者多为老年人。

确诊后不久，品特就去伦敦皇家马斯登医院做手术，清除喉部癌细胞。手术很成功，他将手术成功归功于外科医生的精湛医术，当然还有妻子的悉心照料。

"To survive this kind of disease, you need a brilliant surgeon and a brilliant wife. I was lucky enough to have both," he told a reporter.

He began chemotherapy[1] not long after the operation. As with many patients, he found that the chemotherapy sapped[2] his energy. Later, he spoke of his cancer and its treatment as a personal nightmare. He found chemotherapy "lowering and debilitating[3]".

His creativity was still apparent even during his illness. He wrote the poem "Cancer Cells" while he was undergoing chemotherapy. The source of the poem was a comment made by a nurse at the Royal Marsden Hospital. While she was getting him ready for his chemotherapy one day, she said, "Cancer cells are cells that have forgotten how to die."

This chance remark struck Pinter forcefully. He started writing the poem "Cancer Cells" that same day. In it are these powerful lines:

1. chemotherapy : *n.* 化疗
2. sap : *v.* 逐渐消耗(某人的力量、活力等)
3. debilitating : *adj.* 使虚弱，使衰弱，使丧失能力

> But I remember how to die
> Though all my witnesses are dead.
> But I remember what they said
> Of tumours which would render them

"得这种病，要想不死，得有个医术精湛的医生和体贴的妻子。很幸运，我二者兼得，"他告诉记者。

术后不久，他开始化疗。和许多患者一样，他发现化疗很伤元气。后来他说癌症和治疗对个人来说是场噩梦。他觉得化疗"让人受挫，让人无力"。

即使生病期间，品特仍显示出不凡的创造力。化疗期间，他写了题为《癌细胞》的诗。该诗源自皇家马斯登医院护士的一句话。就在品特准备化疗的那天，护士说，"癌细胞是那些忘了如何死去的细胞。"

说者无心，听者有意。这话语让品特印象深刻。他当天就开始创作《癌细胞》这首诗，诗中有这些逼动的诗句：

> 证人都已死去
> 我却记得怎样死亡
> 我却记得他们说过
> 肿瘤给他们带来的

As blind and dumb as they had been
Before the birth of that disease
Which brought the tumour into play.

Talking to journalist Ramona Koval on the radio show, "Books and Writing", on Radio National and Radio Australia, at the Edinburgh International Book Festival, Pinter said that having the cancer was like a dark dream. He compared his feelings right after his surgery as like being underwater without knowing how to swim. He said he felt disoriented[1]. He didn't know where he was, or even what he was.

He relied on his wife to take care of him during this awful period and help him through safely. She researched his medical condition and made sure that he got the best care. She helped him with his diet. Most of all, she helped him keep his spirits up.

Pinter said he thought the cancer changed him. He felt more conscious of death. He also felt more detached[2]. In talking about his feelings, he noted that no one can really know what it is like to experience catastrophe[3] except those who are suffering it. In his interview with Koval, he talked about the

1. disoriented: *adj.* 迷失，分不清目标或方向
2. detached: *adj.* 超脱
3. catastrophe: *n.* 灾祸，大灾难

盲目和愚钝
一如引发肿瘤的那疾病
产生之前

爱丁堡国际图书节期间，在澳大利亚全国广播公司记者拉蒙娜·科瓦尔的广播节目"书籍和写作"中，品特说得了癌症就像在做黑暗的梦。他将手术后的感受比作在水下而不会游泳，他感到茫重，不知身在何处，甚至不知自己是谁。

这段糟糕的日子里，他靠妻子的照顾，平安渡过难关。她研究品特的病情，确保他得到最好的照料，还安排他的饮食。最重要的是，她让品特保持积极的心态。

品特说癌症改变了他。他对死亡的感觉更为清醒，也更觉超脱。谈到他的感受，他说除非切身体会，否则没人知道经历灾难的感受。

bombing of Iraqi women and children. He said that, since the cancer, he'd realized more clearly the limits of his imagination. Even though he'd been through the blitz and seen bombs dropping, he hadn't seen anyone killed by the bombs.

In spite of his greater awareness of death, Pinter wasn't scared into changing his beliefs about religion. He remained a secularist[1]. Not a Christian, neither did he subscribe to the Jewish faith. Since his bar mitzvah years ago, when he was a boy, he'd gone to a synagogue[2] to attend a wedding now and then. He claimed he didn't remember any part of the Torah[3] he'd studied as a boy.

The cancer was terrible, but more diseases followed it. After the cancer he found he'd contracted a rare auto-immune disease. This disease, pemphigus[4], causes blisters to form on the skin, especially the mucous membranes[5] in the mouth and throat. It tends to occur more often in people of Jewish or Middle Eastern descent, but it attacks people of all races and ethnic groups. This disorder can result in infections in the open sores left when the blisters burst. It is painful and dangerous. In its worst form, it kills ninety percent of its victims. The medications, often steroids[6], used to treat pemphigus can cause bad side effects. Pinter

1. secularist: *n.* 世俗论者，非信仰宗教者
2. synagogue: *n.* 犹太教教堂
3. Torah: *n.*《圣经·旧约》前五卷，又称摩西五经
4. pemphigus: *n.* (医学) 天疱疮
5. mucous membranes: *n.* 黏膜
6. steroids: *n.* 类固醇

在科瓦尔的采访中，品特谈到伊拉克的妇女儿童遭受的轰炸。他说自癌症以来，他才更加意识到想象的局限。他虽见识过闪电战的炸弹，但并没亲眼见过有人被炸弹炸死。

品特对死亡有了更深的认识，但并未因害怕而改变对宗教的看法。他仍是世俗主义者，他不是基督徒，也不信犹太教。自从犹太成年礼以后，他只是偶尔去犹太教堂参加婚礼。他声称已经不记得小时候学的摩西五经了。

癌症很糟糕，更多的疾病随之而来。癌症后，他发现自己得了稀有的自身免疫病。这种病又叫天疱疮，主要引起嘴和喉咙黏膜的皮肤水泡。这种病多发于犹太人或中东人后裔中，但是其他族群也可能染上。水泡破裂后，痛处常会感染。该病既痛苦又危险，最严重的天疱疮致死率高

suffered severe pain in his legs because of medication given to treat this skin disease after his throat cancer had been treated.

That he survived these diseases as long as he did is a testament to his physical stamina[1] and to the devoted care Antonia gave him. He and Antonia had many happy years together before he became ill. They had happy times together afterward, despite his poor health. He continued to be her "first reader" as she worked on biographies. She continued to read his drafts of poems, too. She told reporters that he didn't show his famous anger toward her. She thought reporters exaggerated this trait. She also said he wasn't as competitive as he was reported to be — except in cricket.

They enjoyed each other's company. When they wanted to be alone to focus on a project, each worked in a separate space. Pinter worked in a two-story house behind their Holland Park home. There he had an office on the first floor. His study was on the second floor. In his study was a vibrant portrait of him in an aggressive stance, ready to swing his cricket bat. In the downstairs office were some of his awards. Because of its timing, one of those awards had special meaning for him. He'd been

---

1. stamina *n.* 精力，毅力，持久力

达 90%。治疗天疱疮的类固醇药物有严重的副作用。品特服药期间，腿部剧痛。

品特得了这些病能活下来，显示了他体力之强，也说明了安东尼娅对他照顾之细致。得病前，他和安东尼娅愉快地过了许多年。得病后，尽管品特身体虚弱，他们仍很快乐。她写传记时，品特一直是她的"第一位读者"。她也读品特诗作的初稿。她告诉记者，外界盛传品特脾气如何如何坏，她倒是没有见识过。她认为记者将这个脾气夸大了。另外，她说除了板球比赛以外，品特并不像记者们报道地那样好胜。

他们喜欢在一起。需要各自专心做事时，他们会在各自单独的地方工作。品特在荷兰公园的住宅后一座两层楼的房子里工作。他在一楼有间办公室，书房在二楼。品特书房里有一幅他挥舞板球棒的画像，画像上的他斗志昂扬。楼下办公室里摆着他获得的奖品。一件奖品因为授予时间特殊，对他有着非同寻常的意义。品特出院两天后，被授予英国名

awarded England's Companion of Honor[1] two days after he got out of the hospital from his surgery. This award cheered him and Antonia when they badly needed cheering. Earlier, he'd been offered a knighthood. He'd rejected this offer, saying he didn't want to be honored by his government. The Companion of Honor award, he said, was from his country, for which he felt affection. It wasn't just from the government. He also rejected the offer of knighthood because he thought "Sir Harold" sounded silly. He didn't want to be called "Sir".

Antonia's office is on the fourth floor of their home. She moved into the house in 1959. It was the house her children grew up in. By the time Pinter was ill, the two of them had lived there together for over twenty years. Her study is decorated like an old-fashioned country-house bedroom, except for the business-like office chair and metal filing cabinets. The couch is upholstered with a bright, flowered print; drapes of the same fabric adorn the window above her desk.

The two of them continued to write during Pinter's illness. In 2005, however, he announced that he wouldn't write any more plays. When people protested, he asked whether twenty-nine plays weren't enough for him to have written. He had

1. Companion of Honor: 名誉勋位是英国和英联邦的一种勋章。由英皇乔治五世于1917年6月创设，用以表彰在艺术、音乐、文学、自然科学、政治、工业和宗教方面获得重大成就的人士。

勋勋位。此时夫妇二人急需受到些激励，这个荣誉让他和安东尼娅大受鼓舞。在那之前，他拒绝被封勋爵，他说不想要政府的荣誉。而名誉勋位是国家授予的，让他感受到关爱，而这不仅仅来自于政府。他拒绝爵士头衔，也是因为他觉得"哈罗德爵士"听起来很傻，他不愿被人称作"爵士"。

安东尼娅的办公室在他们家的四楼。她1959年搬进这座房子，她的孩子就是在那长大的。到品特生病时，两人已经在那住了二十多年。除了办公椅和铁制档案橱柜之外，她的书房就像个旧式乡村卧室，沙发用鲜亮的花纹装饰，书桌旁的窗帘也用同样的织物装饰。

品特生病期间，两人仍旧坚持写作。2005年，品特宣布封笔。人们向他抗议时，他就反问难道29部剧本还不够吗？他决定在剩下的日子专

decided to focus on poetry and political activities during the years he had left.

Antonia Fraser continued to write, as she could, while her husband was ill. One of her books, *Marie Antoinette: The Journey*, was made into a film in 2006. The movie is pretty and pastel[1], a confection[2] for the eyes. That same year saw publication of her biography, *Love and Louis the XIV*[3]: *The Women in the Life of the Sun King*. As usual, the book was well-researched and well-written. It has an abundance of stories of ordinary love and affection in that artificial court. As the mother of six, and grandmother of seventeen children, as a wife and lover, Antonia was mostly a great success, full of good-spirited energy. She was at the bedside of her first husband, Hugh Fraser, when he died. She was Harold Pinter's solace and inspiration during his illness and until his death. With all of this, she was lucky enough to be happy and healthy. She had the energy to continue her own writing. Pinter, a remarkable man, had mar-

1. pastel: *adj.* 彩色蜡笔画的，柔和的
2. confection: *n.* 精致工艺品
3. *Louis the XIV*: 路易十四 (1638 – 1715)，自号太阳王，是法国波旁王朝著名的国王，执政期从 1643 年至 1715 年，是世界上执政时间最长的君主之一。路易十四在法国建立了一个君主专制的王国，使其成为当时欧洲最强大的国家和文化中心

心写诗并参加政治活动。

丈夫生病期间，安东尼娅·弗雷泽仍坚持写作。她的作品《旅程：玛丽·安托瓦内特传》于 2006 年被拍成电影，电影拍得很美，如彩笔画一般，是一种视觉享受。她的传记《路易十四情史》也于同年出版。一如往常，该书资料翔实，文笔流畅，书里讲述了那个矫饰的宫廷发生的许多平常的恋爱故事。作为 6 个孩子的母亲和 17 个孩子的祖母，作为妻子和爱人，安东尼娅都颇成功，她总是兴致勃勃，精力充沛。前夫休·弗雷泽逝世时，她一直在床边陪伴。哈罗德·品特生病和逝世时，她给品特安慰和鼓励。她很忙，但幸运的是，她能保持愉快的心情和健康的身体，有精力坚持写作。作为一个杰出的男人，品特有幸娶过两位极富

ried two remarkable women, both extraordinarily talented. No one can know how Vivien would've held up under the duress[1] of his illness. It is clear, however, that his second wife saw him through his terrible ordeal[2] with practical aid and a loving spirit.

1. duress: *n.* 胁迫，压力
2. ordeal: *n.* 严酷的考验，折磨

才华的杰出女性。品特生病期间若是维维恩在身边会是什么情形，我们不得而知。不过，品特的第二任妻子却在品特受折磨期间给了他实际的帮助和关爱。

Chapter Seventeen

HUMOR AND THE ABSURD

幽默与荒诞

*I*t's been said of Harold Pinter that, "if you don't agree with him, you'd better leave the room." This comment implies that he'll make life unpleasant for you if you stay and disagree with him. He has been described in the press as "prickly[1]", "explosive", "egotistical[2]", and "competitive". His wife and his friends counter such descriptions of his personality with their own descriptions of the man. They describe him as warm, generous, and loyal to people he cares about. An old friend even refers to him as "innocent", in his delight in a positive response to his first play, "The Room".

It is understandably tempting for reporters to stick a label on any celebrity. Referring to Britain's most famous playwright as "Mr. Angry", as a headline writer for one newspaper does, helps sell papers. Such language has a sensational appeal. However, Harold Pinter was a complex person. He may have been all of the negative things the press said he was, but these adjectives don't sum him up. They create a caricature. Their result is a cartoon of the man, rather than a realistic portrait of him.

A more balanced description must include other of his salient[3] qualities. One other trait, commonly mentioned in reference to his dramas rather

1. prickly: *adj.* 多刺的
2. egotistical: *adj.* 自私的
3. salient: *adj.* 突出的，显著的

人们评价哈罗德·品特时说，"如果你不同意他的观点，最好离开房间。"这话暗示，如果你不同意他的观点却还留着没走，他会让你很不舒服。媒体形容品特"说话带刺"、"脾气暴躁"、"自我中心"、"争强好胜"。然而，品特的妻子和朋友则有着自己的描述。他们形容品特热心、慷慨、对其所在乎的朋友很忠诚。一位老朋友在称赞品特的第一部戏《房间》时，甚至说他"天真无邪"。

记者喜欢给名人贴标签并不难理解。一份报纸将品特这位英国最著名的剧作家称作"生气先生"，这样做能使报纸畅销。这种说法很有诱惑力。不过，哈罗德·品特性格复杂。如记者所言，他可能有很多坏毛病，但是这些词语并不能反映他的全部。记者的描述像是讽刺画，但那只是漫画，而不是逼真的肖像。

更全面的描述应该包含他性格中的其他突出特点。品特的显著特性之一——人们常用来形容他的戏剧而非他的个性——是其幽默感。品特

than in reference to his personality, is his sense of humor. Pinter has been described as a "cross between Groucho Marx[1] and T.S. Eliot[2]". This comment takes into account the broad, but clever humor of the great Jewish comic, one of the famous Marx brothers, who got their start in Vaudeville[3]. Groucho Marx, the most popular of the brothers, worked in film, radio, and television from the 1920s through the 1950s. Known for his moustache, his big cigar, and his dry wit, toward the end of his career, he was emcee[4] for his own quiz show, "The Grouch Marx Show". The comparison of Pinter's humor to T.S. Eliot's work notes a poetic subtlety of the humor and pathos[5] of the human condition. As represented in the vision of Eliot, an American poet who became an English citizen, it is manifest in the tragicomic poem, "The Love Song of J. Alfred Prufrock". This poem describes a man who is afraid to live — a man who has been so timid and over-careful, that he says he has measured his life "in coffee spoons".

1. Groucho Marx：格劳乔·马克斯 (Julius Henry Groucho Marx, 1890–1977)。美国的喜剧演员、电影明星。他以机智问答及比喻闻名，与家族成员马克斯兄弟合作拍摄了 15 部电影，并且自己的成绩也十分耀眼，担任广播及著名电视节目 You Bet Your Life 主持人。
2. T.S. Eliot：T·S·艾略特 (Thomas Stearns Eliot, 1888-1965)，美国 (1927 年加入英国国籍) 诗人、评论家、剧作家，有诗集《普鲁弗洛克及其他》(Prufrock and Other Observations, 1917)、《诗选》(Poems, 1919)、《四个四重奏》(Four Quartets, 1943) 等。艾略特因"革新现代诗，功绩卓著"而获 1948 年诺贝尔奖文学奖。
3. Vaudeville：n. 歌舞杂耍
4. emcee：n. 主持, 支持人
5. pathos：n. 感伤, 痛苦

被称作"格劳乔·马克斯和 T·S·艾略特的交集"。该评论提到了身材高大、幽默机智的伟大犹太戏剧演员、以歌舞杂耍起家的马克斯兄弟之一格劳乔·马克斯。格劳乔·马克斯是所有兄弟中最出名的，从 20 世纪 20 年代到 50 年代一直制作电影、广播和电视节目。马克斯因其胡须、大雪茄和机智出名。在其事业末期，他是智力竞猜节目《格劳乔·马克斯秀》的主持人。将品特的幽默和艾略特的作品相提并论，说明品特的幽默有种微妙的诗意，还有对人类处境的感伤。艾略特这位美国诗人(后加入英国国籍)的想象都表现在悲喜剧诗歌《J·阿尔弗瑞德·普鲁弗洛克的情歌》里。这首诗描写了一个害怕活着的男人——他胆小，过于谨慎，说自己用"咖啡勺"计量生活。普鲁弗洛克的恐惧

Prufrock's fear made him incapable of meaningful action. Pinter was determined not to succumb[1] to such fear. That such fear would have been tempting to a man who was a child during the holocaust, during which millions of Jews were murdered, is likely. His plays are, in a sense, both expressions of this kind of fear and an antidote[2] to it.

Pinter himself said his favorite comedian was Jack Benny[3]. Like Grouch Marx, Jack Benny was a Jewish-American comic who got his start in Vaudeville. Interestingly, Benny made his long pauses an important element in his humor. Pinter said he thought about his own use of pauses as coming in part from hearing Jack Benny. Another element in Benny's humor was the exaggeration of his own stinginess[4] and vanity. For example, after he got old enough that the lie was apparent, Jack Benny insisted to his audiences that he was only thirty-nine years old.

Surely of great importance to Pinter's personality, as well as his work is his Jewish working-class origins. An anecdote[5] that he told about an incident from his boyhood suggests the significance of these origins.

1. succumb: *v.* 屈服，服从
2. antidote: *n.* 解毒药，解毒剂
3. Jack Benny: 杰克·班尼 (1894–1974) 是美国喜剧演员、歌舞杂耍演员和广播电视电影演员
4. stinginess: *n.* 小气
5. anecdote: *n.* 轶闻，趣事

使他无法做出有意义的举动。品特决心不向这种恐惧屈服。童年生活在杀死几百万犹太人的大屠杀的时期，这种恐惧本会使他屈服。某种程度上说，品特的戏剧既表现了这种恐惧，又提供了破解之术。

品特说他最喜爱的喜剧演员是杰克·班尼。和格劳乔·马克斯一样，杰克·班尼也是犹太裔美国喜剧演员，也以歌舞杂耍起家。有趣的是，班尼常用停顿作为自己幽默的重要元素。品特说他之所以用长时间的停顿，部分原因是听了杰克·班尼的台词。班尼的另一幽默元素是夸大自己的小气和虚荣。比如，当杰克·班尼已经明显老了，无法佯装年轻时，却仍坚持告诉观众他只有39岁。

品特犹太工人阶层的出身，肯定对他的个性和作品起到了至关重要的作用。品特透露了一件童年的轶事，显示了他成长背景对自己的影响。

One day the young Pinter went to visit his father, Jack, at the tailor shop where Jack worked. Lunchtime had just ended, and father and son were still talking when Jack's boss yelled at him to get back to work. Harold Pinter made a rude gesture toward the boss. Seeing the gesture, Jack slapped young Harold in the face, hard.

"I have to work here," said Jack to his son.

This incident surely had a dramatic effect on Pinter's feelings about himself and his father. He must have felt ashamed and angry, as well as hurt. These feelings, stemming from seeing his father treated impolitely, seeing his father accept such treatment and even — in a sense — betraying himself and his son by punishing his son for refusing such treatment of his father, would have been turbulent[1] for most adolescents.

If Pinter hadn't already decided that he'd be his own man, surely that incident helped him to arrive at that important decision.

Pinter's father might have explained his own behavior by saying that in punishing his son, he was ensuring that his son understand the realities of working-class life. However, he must have been happy, later on, to find that his son was able to defy those realities.

1. turbulent: *adj.* 狂躁的，暴躁的

一天，年轻的品特去父亲杰克工作的缝纫店找他。午餐时间结束后，父子俩仍在谈话，杰克的老板喊他回去工作。哈罗德·品特朝老板做了个粗鲁的手势。杰克看见这个手势后，重重地打了哈罗德一记耳光。

"我还得在这里做事呢，"杰克对儿子说。

这件事一定对品特父子的感情有戏剧化的影响。他感到羞耻和愤怒，也受到伤害。有这些感觉，是因为父亲对自己的粗鲁，是因为他看见了父亲忍受这样的待遇，也是因为他看到父亲在一定程度上背叛了他自己和儿子，仅仅因儿子不能接受他所遭到的待遇而去惩罚他。这些感情对大部分青少年来说都很有刺激性。

如果说此前品特尚未独立自主的话，这件事一定促使他做出"凡事靠自己"这个重要决定了。

品特的父亲后来可能为其行为向儿子解释过，跟儿子说这也是为了让他认清工人阶层的生活现实。不过，后来发现儿子能够挑战现实，他一定很开心。

Pinter's humor showed his awareness of the forces aligned against anyone's success in living a good life. His plays were described as "black comedies" and as "comedies of menace" because they combined humor with the implied violence behind the ordinary routines of life. In "Ashes to Ashes", for example, a man is visited by an old friend and the old friend's girlfriend. The old friend and girlfriend strip naked and get into the man's bed. The humor behind this bizarre behavior is that it builds on the real fear that things will get out of control. Powerful forces like sexual feelings and violent impulses threaten to upset the compromises that people make to maintain an equilibrium[1] that allows them to fulfill the roles they've created to get by in the world.

Pinter's sense of humor has been called wicked because it is sly[2] in showing the masks people put on to hide their vulnerability to such forces. He often uses clichés to point out the uselessness of such masks. In the dramatic situation of the play, the cliché shows itself as ridiculously inadequate or irrelevant, or both.

Pinter has been quoted as saying that everything is funny, even tragedy.

1. equilibrium: *n.* 平衡，均衡
2. sly: *adj.* 狡猾的

从品特的幽默中能看出，他意识到一个人想过好日子，冥冥中总会有什么力量在和这人作梗。他的戏剧被称为"黑色喜剧"和"胁迫剧"，因为他将幽默和日常生活背后所隐藏的暴力结合起来了。比如，在《烬于尘土终于尘土》中，一男人的老友携女友来访，这位老友和女友脱得精光，上了他的床。这种行为看似怪异，背后的幽默却是一种恐惧，一种对事态失控的真实恐惧。性和暴力冲动威胁到人们为了平衡而作的各种妥协。而正是这样的平衡，让人可以按照自我营造的角色，生活在这个世上。

品特的幽默感被人视为不道德，因为它狡猾地揭示了人们戴着的虚假面具，以及靠这种面具所掩饰的各自在上述力量之前的软弱处。他常用陈词滥调来指出这类面具的无用。在戏剧场景中，这种陈词滥调显得轻薄之至、无益之至，或是二者兼有。

据称，品特说过，所有事物都可笑，即便悲剧也是如此。

"The greatest earnestness is funny; even tragedy is funny," he says, but goes on to say that tragedy reaches a point when it is no longer funny. This remark shows Pinter as belonging to an existentialist[1] trend of thought that was popular after World War II and into the 1960s. Modern existentialist thinkers, most of them atheists[2], such as Jean-Paul Sartre[3], wrote that life has no intrinsic meaning[4] because there is no supernatural power to give it meaning. Essentially, life is absurd and pointless. Though this view is considered pessimistic by many people, it also offers an optimistic alternative to belief in God. That alternative is a belief that humans can make their lives meaningful by their own actions. Committing to something they believe is worthwhile is one way of making meaning, according to this view.

1. existentialist: *adj.* 存在主义的。存在主义（Existentialism），又称生存主义，是一种哲学的非理性主义思潮，强调个人、独立自主和主观经验。叔本华（Arthur Schopenhauer, 1788–1860）、尼采（Friedrich Wilhelm Nietzsche, 1844–1900）和索伦·克尔凯郭尔（Søren Kierkegaard, 1813–1855）是其先驱。存在主义在20世纪流传非常广泛，其哲学思想还延续到了60年代兴起的人本主义（Humanism）。雅斯贝尔斯（Karl Jaspers, 1883–1969）和马丁·海德格尔（Martin Heidegger, 1889–1976）、保罗·萨特（Jean-Paul Sartre, 1905–1980）和作家阿尔贝·加缪（Albert Camus, 1913–1960）是其代表人物。
2. atheists: *n.* 无神论者
3. Jean-Paul Sartre: 让-保罗·萨特（1905–1980）是法国存在主义哲学家、剧作家、小说家，其代表作《存在与虚无》（*L'être et le néant*, 1943）是存在主义的巅峰之作。
4. intrinsic meaning: *n.* 内在意义

"最大的诚意也是好笑的；即便悲剧也是好笑的，"他说，但他接着又说悲剧到一定程度就不再好笑。这说明品特属于二战后至60年代期间流行起来的存在主义思潮。现代存在主义思想家大都是无神论者，比如让-保罗·萨特，他曾写道，生命没有内在意义，因为没有超自然力量赋予生命意义。本质上说，生命是荒诞无意义的。尽管很多人认为这观点很悲观，但该观点也提供了一个除了"信仰上帝"以外的乐观选择。这个选择就是相信人类能通过自己的行动，让生命变得有意义。依照这种观点，从事某些认为值得做的事，是使生命变得有意义的一种途径。

Chapter Eighteen

CRICKET

板球缘

*A*t an early age, Pinter committed himself to living by his own standards. This meant refusing to do what he was told if it violated his own sense of what he should do. It also meant dedicating himself to his art. Early on, it informed his enthusiasm for cricket.

"Cricket is the greatest thing God ever invented. Better than sex, though sex isn't too bad," he said to Ramona Koval during their radio interview at the Edinburgh International Book Festival in 2002. She asked him why he liked cricket so much when he generally didn't like rules.

"There are some good rules, fair rules," said Pinter.

Sports like cricket, in England, and basketball and football, in the United States, are areas of endeavor where social class doesn't matter so much. Poor children can excel in[1] one of these sports if they start young enough, have talent, and play hard. Playing these sports doesn't take a lot of money, as do sports that generally require private lessons, such as golf or tennis.

Too, these sports are an acceptable outlet for aggression. In playing cricket, Pinter could struggle and succeed in a physical fight that didn't hurt anyone. In fact, since cricket is a national sport, he was

1. excel in: v.在…方面胜过，超过

品特年轻时就立志按自己的标准生活。这意味着拒绝做有悖于自己意愿的事，这还意味着献身于艺术。在早期，这种执着体现在他对板球的热情上。

"板球是上帝最伟大的发明。板球比性生活还好，不过性这东西也不坏，" 2002年爱丁堡国际图书节期间，品特在接受拉蒙娜·科瓦尔广播采访时这样说。拉蒙娜·科瓦尔问品特，既然他平素不喜规则，为何又对板球如此热衷？

"有些规则是好的规则，是公平的规则。" 品特说。

板球在英国，就像篮球和橄榄球在美国一样，不论社会阶层，谁都能参与。只要练得早，有天分，肯努力，穷孩子在这些运动上也可以有出色表现。不像高尔夫或网球这些通常需要私人教练的运动，板球之类的运动不需要花很多钱。

这些运动还可以一种社会认可的方式，释放人的进攻性。板球运动中，品特可以争斗，可以打败别人，却又不造成伤害。其实，板球为英

admired for playing. Cricket is almost as patriotic[1], or thoroughly English, a game, as baseball is thoroughly American. Cricket has been popular in England since at least the 1600s. Both cricket and baseball derive from[2] earlier games of prowess[3], with fewer rules and rougher play.

   Once he started playing the game, Pinter was as loyal to cricket as he was to his boyhood friends. After his dramatic success, when his time was in great demand, he belonged to a cricket club, the Gaieties. In his thirty years with the Gaieties Cricket Club, he earned a reputation for being an excellent player. His knowledge of the game was encyclopedic[4].

   Though Pinter played squash[5] and tennis, too, cricket was the sport he'd loved as a child. After all, he'd carried his cricket bat with him every time he evacuated his home during the blitz. In a world in which strength and power often manifest themselves in brutality, cricket offered a place where strength and power could manifest themselves in admirable fair play and athletic grace. In his imagination, cricket recalled times that were, if not golden, at least tinged with glory.

1. patriotic: *adj.* 爱国的，有爱国心的
2. derive from: *v.* 从…衍生而来
3. prowess: *n.* 威力
4. encyclopedic: *adj.* 知识全面的，百科全书式的
5. squash: *n.* 壁球

国全国性运动，参加板球比赛他反倒会受人钦佩。如同美国人打棒球一样，板球在英国被视为一项爱国的运动，或曰纯粹的英国式运动。自 1600 年起，该运动就开始在英国流行。板球和棒球都是由一些规则比较少、玩法更简单的早期力量型比赛演化而来。

   开始玩板球后，品特就像忠实于童年伙伴一样，忠于这项运动。在戏剧生涯获得成功后，他虽然繁忙，但还是加入了盖蒂斯板球俱乐部。在 30 年的俱乐部生活中，品特赢得了杰出板球手的声誉。他对这项运动无所不通。

   品特也打壁球和网球，但板球是他自孩提时代就热爱的运动。闪电战期间，他从家疏散的时候都不忘带上板球棒。在一个能力、实力常表现为蛮力暴力的世界中，板球提供了一个平台，让他能够通过公平竞争和运动员的风度，展示自己的能量和实力。在他的想象中，板球让人回想到了光辉岁月，甚至可说是黄金时代。

An old saying, when someone violates any rule, is "that's not cricket[1]". This saying holds cricket up as a standard for fairness and behaving correctly toward others. The game, with all its rules, is a symbol for order and justice.

Pinter stood up for[2] himself. Being Jewish and coming from a working-class family, it took a lot more courage to stand up for himself than it would've had he come from a mainstream background of privilege. More than other men of his accomplishments, he felt he had to keep his guard up. He could relax with his friends and family, but with the public, he was often ready for a fight.

In talking with Koval, he mentions how he'd been ready for an argument when he landed in the airport in Miami, Florida, as he was traveling back from a political trip to Nicaragua. He walked up to customs expecting the U.S. official there to question what he'd been doing in Nicaragua. He had his response all planned. He intended to say to the official, "It's none of your business". He was surprised and disconcerted when the woman at the customs desk asked him if he was *the* Harold Pinter. He said he was.

1. not cricket: *adj.* 不光明磊落的，不公正的
2. stand up for: 公开支持或拥护某人或事业

有这样一句谚语，当人们破坏某项规则，大家会说 "那可不是在打板球啊(即不光明磊落)"。该谚语将板球当做公正对待他人的一个楷模。这项崇尚规则的运动，正是秩序和公正的象征。

品特知道如何捍卫自己。作为来自工人阶层的犹太人，比起来自主流特权阶层的那些人而言，捍卫自己需要更大的勇气。作为一个成就斐然的人，他觉得需要自我保护。和家人朋友在一起他会很轻松，但是面对公众，他就会随时准备战斗。

在和科瓦尔的谈话中，他谈到从尼加拉瓜政治之旅返回时，到了佛罗里达这阿密机场，就抱着和人斗嘴的念头。他走向海关，以为美国官员会质询他在尼加拉瓜的所作所为。他已经计划好了如何回答。他准备对官员说，"和你无关。"当海关办公桌边的女官员问他是否正是哈罗德·品特时，他回答说是。

"Welcome to the United States," she said, with a smile.

The impression this incident made on Pinter suggests that he was glad to have been greeted so warmly. He didn't need it, but he was glad for it.

Friendship meant a lot to him. He could even enjoy being the butt of his friends' jokes occasionally. He liked telling about a performance of "The Birthday Party", in which he played the role of Stanley. He had cast his old friend, Patrick McGee, in this production of the play. He and McGee had been young actors together, long before in Ireland. They'd been friends since those early days in their career. During this particular performance of "The Birthday Party", Pinter and McGee were on stage, in dialogue together. When Pinter hesitated, forgetting his lines, McGee just looked at him and smiled a devilish smile. McGee thought it was funny that the playwright had forgotten his own lines. He stood there enjoying Pinter's discomfort and refused to help him. Pinter liked McGee's sense of humor in leaving him to struggle in embarrassment. He could see the delight McGee took in the playwright's forgetting his own lines — lines he'd written for Stanley, one of the most famous characters in one of his most famous plays.

"欢迎来美国，"她笑着说。

这件事令他惊讶也给品特留下了印象，说明他很乐于受到这样热情的欢迎。这样的热情虽然并非不可或缺，但却使他颇为高兴。

友谊对品特很重要。他甚至乐意偶尔在朋友的笑话中成为笑柄。他喜欢说某一次《生日晚会》演出的事，剧中他扮演斯坦利。他让老朋友帕特里克·麦吉在剧中扮演角色。老早以前，两人都还年轻的时候，同在爱尔兰做演员，从那时起两人就是事业上的朋友。在这场《生日晚会》的演出中，品特和麦吉在舞台上有段对话。品特忘了台词，麦吉看着他，有些狡猾地笑了笑，他为哈罗德忘记自己写的台词而感到好笑。他站在那里，幸灾乐祸地看着品特在那里尴尬，却并不去提醒帮助。麦吉这种任他尴尬的做法表现了他的幽默感，品特很喜欢。他看得出麦吉见他忘了台词而感到好笑。他忘的是他最著名的一部剧中为最著名的角色斯坦利所写的台词。

Pinter told Carey Perloff, when he visited her rehearsals for "The Birthday Party" and "Mountain Language" in New York, about a joke made by his friend Samuel Beckett. He told Perloff that during a visit to see Beckett, Pinter happened to mention that he was depressed about the state of the world.

"Not as depressed as I am, Harold," quipped[1] Beckett.

Pinter appreciated Beckett's joke because it admitted the basic competitiveness of both men. They were friends, but both wanted to be great writers. A part of each man wanted to be the *greatest* writer. Beckett was suggesting, lightheartedly, that he had Pinter beaten, even in depression.

The kinds of "one-upmanship[2]" that he could appreciate in the context of a friendship were like the competition in cricket, based on a mutual understanding of the rules of the game. In Pinter's creative writing, cricket and friendship are closely allied. This is most clear in his play, "No Man's Land", written in 1974. Several characters in the play are named for famous cricket players: Spooner, Hirst, Foster, and Briggs. This play, one of Pinter's most haunting and poetic works, is criticized as obscure even after many of his other works have won acclaim. The title harks back to that part of the west-

1. quip: *v.* 说出妙语或讽刺话
2. one-upmanship: *n.* 胜人一筹

在他因《生日晚会》和《山地语言》的彩排而访问纽约期间，品特跟凯莉·珀洛夫讲了好友塞缪尔·贝克特的一个笑话。他告诉珀洛夫，他去看贝克特时，品特偶尔提到世界局势让他郁闷。

"不会比我更郁闷，哈罗德，"贝克特亚贫嘴。

品特欣赏贝克特的笑话，因为它承认了两人之间的竞争。他们是朋友，但两人都想成为伟大作家，甚至成为最伟大的作家。贝克特漫不经心地暗示，甚至在郁闷上，他都要打败品特。

他在友谊中所欣赏的比拼，如同板球比赛一样，是建立在双方对运动规则的共识上。在品特的创作中，板球和友谊紧密相关。这在品特1974年的剧本《无人地带》里表现得最明显。剧中一些人物都取了著名板球运动员的名字：斯普纳，赫斯特，福斯特和布里格斯。这部戏是品特最吸引人、最有诗意的作品，但即便在其它几部作品赢得赞誉之后，该作品仍被评为太过晦涩。该剧的标题让人想起第一次世界大战时西线的

ern front in World War I referred to as "no man's land" because so few could trespass it and live. Between the trenches of the German and French armies, machine gun fire sprayed any soldiers ordered across it. The title implies a battlefield that no one can survive — even great heroes, like England's cricketers — no matter how bravely or desperately they fight.

Like almost everyone, Pinter cared what people thought of him. He tried not to let their opinion matter so much that it made him act differently than he thought he should. Part of Pinter's reputation for being cruelly blunt may have come from his determination to be his own person. To tell a lie is cowardly. His wife said she'd never known him to tell even a fib, much less a lie. He must sometimes have had to steel himself to tell the truth, just as he had to steel himself at times to face his public.

In his essay, "Writing for the Theatre", he talks about an opening night of "The Caretaker" in Düsseldorf, Germany. At the end of the play, when he took his bow with the cast of actors, he was booed[1] loudly. He said later that the boos were so loud he thought the audience had megaphones. Nevertheless, he and the cast took

1. boo: v. 嘘声，喝倒彩

"无人地带"。这是一片很少人能活着闯过的防线。在德法军的战线之间，任何想闯过去的士兵，都会遭到机枪扫射。该标题暗示战场上没人能够活下来——即使是英国板球国手那样的英雄——不论他们作战是何等英勇无畏。

和几乎所有人一样，品特在意别人怎么看自己。他试着不让别人的意见影响自己。品特那种不讲情面的直白是出了名的，其部分原因是他我行我素。说谎是懦夫的行为。品特的妻子说他从来不说谎，甚至连小谎都不说。他有时一定是强令自己说出事实的，正如他强令自己面对大众那样。

在《为剧院写作》一文中，品特谈到《看门人》在德国杜塞尔多夫的首演之夜。演出结束，他和演员一起谢幕，观众大声喝倒彩。他后来说，喝倒彩声很大，他甚至以为观众们用了麦克风。尽管如此，剧组还

thirty-four curtain calls[1] — all the while the audience booed. The memory of this extravaganza[2] of disapproval helped him face later anxieties over whether audiences and reviewers would like his plays.

Many themes in Harold's life weave into a pattern that harks back to one of his most famous lines.

"Don't let them tell you want to do," Petey says to Stanley in "The Birthday Party". Whether orders come from God, the boss, father or mother, obeying them when they are at odds with your own sense of right and wrong means destroying your chances for a good life.

The portrait of Pinter, holding a cricket bat, was put up for auction in 2009 to raise money for a charity sponsored by the Lords Taverners, a cricket charity for children. The painting, by artist Joe Hill, was given to Pinter by his friends. They gave it to him in gratitude for his long service to the Gaieties Cricket Club. With the auction of this painting, the writer's devotion to this English pastime continues.

1. curtain call *n.* 谢幕，要求演员谢幕的掌声和呼声
2. extravaganza *n.* 内容狂妄的作品，狂妄的言行

是 34 次谢幕，其间观众一直喝倒彩。这次被人大喝倒彩的遭遇他牢记在心，日后遇到观众和评论家对剧作的否定，他就不再上心了。

哈罗德生活中的很多主题，都形成了规律，且与其剧作中一些著名台词暗合。

"别让他们对你指手画脚，"《生日晚会》一剧中，佩蒂对斯坦利说。不论是上帝、老板、还是父母，如果遵守他们的要求与自己的是非观相左，就意味着会毁掉你自己过好日子的机会。

2009 年，品特手握板球棒的肖像画被拍卖，以筹集善款资助洛兹·塔佛纳斯基金会——一个致力于儿童事业的板球慈善基金。这画作是乔·希尔所作，是他的朋友送给他的，籍以感谢他对盖蒂斯板球俱乐部的长期支持。通过画作拍卖，作家延续了他对板球这项著名英国式运动的热情。

Chapter Nineteen

NOBEL PRIZE

诺贝尔奖

On October 13, 2005, Pinter got a phone call about twenty minutes before the Swedish Academy made the announcement public. He answered the phone and learned that he had been selected to receive the Nobel Prize in Literature that year. Pinter was surprised. He said he didn't even realize he was a real contender.

He told Antonia the good news. Not long afterward, he took an opportunity to tease her. She loved pretty things.

"Buy a new dress to celebrate the occasion," he said. "But don't spend any more than 700,000 pounds."

They both knew the Nobel Prize award would be 1.3 million dollars, or about seven hundred and thirty thousand pounds. His outrageous proposal that she spend most of the money on a new gown was especially funny in view of Antonia's closet full of beautiful clothes. The joke reflected his exuberant[1] mood. This award came not long after his seventh-fifth birthday. Though he was confident in the value of his life's work, having its worth confirmed by this international award was a wonderful birthday gift.

In citing reasons for its choice, the academy in Stockholm said that Pinter had "restored theatre to its basic elements: an enclosed space and unpredict-

1. exuberant: *adj.* 繁茂的，丰富的

2005 年 10 月 13 日，瑞典文学院公布品特获得诺贝尔文学奖这一消息 20 分钟前，品特接到了电话。电话中，品特得知他获得了当年的诺贝尔文学奖。品特很吃惊，他说甚至没有意识到自己是诺贝尔奖的真正角逐者。

品特把这个好消息告诉安东尼娅。没多久，他又借此机会和爱美的安东尼娅开了个玩笑。

"去买件漂亮的衣服来庆祝一下，"他说，"但是可别超过 70 万英镑。"

他们都知道诺贝尔奖金大约有 130 万美元，折合约 73 万英镑。安东尼娅的衣橱里漂亮衣服琳琅满目，品特让安东尼娅把钱大部分都花在礼服上的提议很是好笑。这玩笑也反映了他有多开心。品特是在 75 岁生日后不久获得诺贝尔奖的。他对自己作品的价值一直有信心，不过得到这个国际大奖的认可，对他来说是绝好的生日礼物。

瑞典文学院公布品特的获奖理由为："使戏剧回归到基本元素：在封

able dialogue, where people are at the mercy of each other and pretence crumbles." The citation also said that he had won recognition as a fighter for human rights and for taking positions that were controversial.

Phone calls from friends and from the press began immediately after the announcement. Still weak from a recent head injury he'd suffered in Dublin, when he slipped on wet pavement and fell, Pinter told reporters that he understood that he was to give a forty-five minute acceptance speech. He said he wasn't sure yet what his speech would be about. He also talked to them about the rare skin disease, painful and unpleasant, affecting his mouth. He mentioned Antonia frequently in his conversations with the press, saying how glad he was to have her as his wife.

"Without her, I couldn't have coped these last few years," he said.

Pinter let the public know that he was moved by this international commendation from the Swedish Academy. He said that in receiving the Nobel Prize, he was in remarkable company.

As with most of the Nobel Prize awards, the news about Pinter's winning the award caused controversy. Most people who gave their opinion publicly thought the award highly deserved. Some, however,

闲的房间和日常闲聊中，伪装粉碎了，人们处在彼此支配下。"获奖理由中还说品特作为人权和有争议问题的斗士，得到了认可。

获奖公布后，品特立刻接到朋友和媒体的电话。之前，品特在都柏林潮湿的人行道上滑倒，头部受伤，当时正在康复，体质虚弱。品特告诉记者说他知道要发表一场45分钟的获奖演说。他说还不知道届时会说什么。他还告诉记者，说自己得了罕见的皮肤病，很痛很不舒服，也影响到了他的嘴巴。在接受媒体采访中，他对安东尼娅赞不绝口，说他有这样的妻子何等幸运。

"没有她，这几年我应付不下来，"他说。

品特说瑞典文学院给他颁发这一国际大奖使他深受感动。他说能和以前那些出色的获奖者为伍，他倍感荣耀。

同大多数诺贝尔奖一样，品特获奖的新闻引发了争议。大多数公开发表意见的人认为品特获奖实至名归。一些人则说品特配不上。不过，

said they thought Pinter didn't deserve the award. However, most people who disagreed with the academy's choice seemed to be angry about Pinter's politics, rather than about his art. Journalist Christopher Hitchens, for example, complained that Pinter's political position against the United States was hysterical[1] . One of the few leftists to support the war against Iraq, Hitchens' use of the word "hysterical" to describe Pinter's opposition to the war may reflect Hitchens' ire[2] at the heavy criticism he himself had faced from many people on the left. At any rate, few detractors[3] could argue that Pinter's body of work was insignificant. They might say they didn't like it, but they couldn't say it was unimportant. Pinter had helped to create a whole new kind of theatre, a theatre that was unmediated[4] by a moralizing nineteenth-century narrative intended to reveal characters' motives and to make judgments about them. Pinter's theatre offered no explanations. It raised disturbing questions. These questions and the silences they amplified resonated[5] with modern audiences. Pinter's audiences had seen films of the walking skeletons[6] released from German concentration camps. They had seen pictures of earth taken from the blackness of space. Because of new tech-

1. hysterical: *adj.* 歇斯底里的
2. ire: *n.* 愤怒
3. detractors: *n.* 诽谤者，中伤者
4. unmediate: *v.* 不调停，没有中介的
5. resonate: *v.* (使) 共鸣，(使) 共振
6. skeleton: *n.* 骨架，骨骼

不赞同瑞典文学院决定的人，大多愤恨的是品特的政治立场，而非他的艺术。比如，记者克里斯托弗·希钦斯抱怨品特的反美政治立场歇斯底里。希钦斯是少数支持伊战的左翼分子之一，他用"歇斯底里"来形容品特的反战立场，或许是因为他自己在左翼阵营里受到许多人的严厉批评而深感恼怒。不论如何，即便批评者，也很难质疑品特作品的重要性。他们或许会说他们不喜欢这些作品，但不能说它们不重要。品特创造了一种新型戏剧，这种戏剧没有 19 世纪戏剧的道德说教，也没有这种戏剧对人物动机的揭示和评判。品特的戏剧里不提供解释，而是提出些令人不安的问题。这些问题和它们所彰显的沉默，能让现代观众产生共鸣。品特的观众见过德军集中营里释放出来的形如骷髅的人。他的观众见过从黑暗太空拍摄的地球照片。由于这些新技术，他们开始认识到人类真

nologies they had begun to recognize the boundlessness of human capacity for evil. They were less sure about human capacity for good; but many people hoped there something could be learned by looking into the void and the desperate, often comic, human struggle to create meaning out of it.

Pinter was expected to talk about his art when he accepted the Nobel Prize for Literature. He was also expected to talk about his political views, as they had become entwined with his art. He knew he was too weak to travel to Stockholm for the award ceremony, but for a time he thought he might go there to deliver his lecture before the day of the ceremony. However, it became clear that he wasn't well enough to travel at all. His speech was recorded in London. He left the hospital to tape the speech, and then returned to the hospital afterward.

The video of his speech was shown on December 7, 2005, in Sweden. In the video, Pinter sits on-stage in a wheelchair. The bare stage with a backdrop[1] of curtains is dimly lit, in blue tones. The only object on the stage is a large black and white photograph of a younger Pinter, dark-haired and vital, dressed casually in slacks and a white open-collared shirt, standing and looking

1. backdrop. *n.* 背景，背景幕布

有无限的作恶能力。他们对人类行善的能力没有那么有把握。但是很多人希望，仰望虚空之时，能从人类为了寻求意义而作的绝望、甚至滑稽的争斗中学到点什么。

接爱诺贝尔文学奖时，人们预计品特会讨论他的艺术。另外，因为他的政治观念和文学创作密不可分，人们也希望听到他的政治见解。品特知道自己身体太虚弱，不能去斯德哥尔摩参加颁奖典礼。也想过自己也许能够去参加典礼，在典礼前一天发表演说。不过，后来他的身体状况实在不好，显然无法成行。他在伦敦录制了获奖演说。录制期间他离开了医院，录后又回到医院。

这段视频演说于 2005 年 12 月 7 日在瑞典播放。录像中，品特坐在舞台上的轮椅里。舞台上很空，背景是幕布，舞台上只有微弱的蓝光。舞台上唯一的道具是品特年轻时的一幅黑白照片。照片上他头发乌黑，充满朝气，身上随意地穿着休闲裤和开领衬衫，站着看着镜头。而品特本

toward the camera. The real Pinter sits with a plaid blanket over his lap. He wears a dark-colored jacket over a black shirt, the shirt collar buttoned at the neck, with no tie. He looks into the camera as he talks, his voice, once so deep, now slightly hoarse[1].

In his acceptance speech, "Art, Truth, and Politics", Pinter begins by talking about truth in art. He reminds his audience that the kind of truth expressed through art can be contradictory. Something can be true and yet its opposite can also be true. He talks about the origin of his plays, saying they almost always come from an imagined word or a line, followed by an image.

"The Homecoming," he says, originated with a line that just came into his head, apparently out of nowhere:

"What have you done with the scissors?"

A single word was the origin of another play.

"Dark". This one word began his work on "Old Times". As he "heard" the word in his mind, he thought of it as an answer to a question about a woman's hair.

In his speech, Pinter tells his audience that when he begins writing his plays he first designates

---

1. hoarse: *adj.* 嗓音嘶哑的，沙哑的

人则坐着，膝上搭着一条格子花呢毯子，身穿黑色衬衫，外套一件黑色夹克。衬衫领一直扣到脖子，脖子上没打领结。他看着镜头说话，过去那深沉的声音如今显得沙哑。

在题为《艺术、真理和政治》的获奖演说中，品特以讨论艺术中的真相开始。他提醒观众，通过艺术表达的真相可能相互矛盾。有些真相是真的，而对立面也是真的。他谈到自己戏剧作品的起源，说他总是最先有个想象的词语或是一句台词，后面跟着一个意象。

他说《归家》一剧就是来自他脑海里突然闪现的一句台词。

"你用剪刀做了什么？"

另一部戏剧始于一个词语。

《昔日》一剧始于"黑暗"一词。他在脑海里"听到"这个词时，还以为它是回答一个关于女人头发的问题。

在演说中，品特告诉观众，当他写剧本时，他首先用"A"、"B"、"C"

the characters with letters, such as "A", "B", and "C". Only later does he name them. The characters don't seem to follow his will; they seem to have a will of their own. The playwright, he says, isn't welcomed by the characters. He talks about his writing process as "fitful[1]".

"Our beginnings never know our ends," he notes.

After discussing truth in art, he contrasts it with truth in politics. He says that, to be good citizens, people must know what is true. In his speech, he expresses his belief that since the end of World War II, the United States has increasingly abused its position of power in the world. He singles out[2] particular instances of its abuse of power. He discusses the Reagan-era policy of training and supporting counter-revolution-aries to overturn the Sandinista government in Nicaragua. This was done, he says, because the United States didn't want an example of a neighboring government that cared more about people than about profit. He speaks, too, about unfounded claims used by President Bush and others to justify invasion of Iraq after Al Qaeda's destruction of the World Trade Towers on September 11, 2001. Pinter made fun of Britain's support of the war on Iraq, calling Britain a "bleating lamb" following along after the United States. He talks

1. fitful: *adj.* 断断续续的，间歇性，突发性的
2. single out: *v.* 挑选

来代指人物。人物并不随他的意愿。他们似有各自的意志。品特说，剧作家并不爱剧中人物的欢迎。他说写作过程具有"突发性"特征。

"开始从来不知道结束时是什么样，"他说。

讨论完艺术中的真相后，他将艺术真相和政治真相进行对比。他说，要想做优秀的公民，人们必须知道真相。演说中，品特说他相信，自二战以来，美国一直在全世界滥用自己的权力。他举了美国滥用权力的例子。他说里根时代美国训练、支持尼加拉瓜反革命武装推翻桑地尼斯塔政府。品特说，美国这样做，是因为美国不想让邻国政府关注人民多于关注利润，从而树立一个他们不希望看到的榜样。他还说，布什总统等人以 2001 年 9 月 11 日世贸大楼被基地组织撞毁为由，入侵了伊拉克。品特嘲笑英国政府支持伊拉克战争，他把英国政府称作"咩咩叫的绵羊"，只会跟着美国走。他谈到了古巴的关塔那摩监狱，那里囚犯全被羁押着

about Guantanamo Bay in Cuba, where prisoners have been held for years without due process of law. He says that President George W. Bush and Prime Minister Tony Blair should be tried for war crimes.

According to Pinter, the majority of politicians aren't interested in the truth.

"They're interested in power," he asserts. For politicians to gain and keep power, he says it is essential that people remain ignorant.

"What surrounds us is a vast tapestry of lies," Pinter says.

In an upper-class accent that contrasts with the cockney slang he employs so effectively in many of his plays, he indicts[1] the United States and Britain for their slaughter of innocent civilians in different parts of the world. He says the United States has supported dictators in Indonesia, Greece, Brazil, Guatemala, the Philippines, and Chile. In phrases that are reminiscent[2] of his plays, he says that though hundreds, even thousands, of innocent people have been killed in these countries and in other places, "nothing ever happened", even while it was happening.

He concludes his speech with two poems, the first, by Pablo Neruda[3], is about the bombing of ci-

1. indict: *v.* 控诉，指控
2. reminiscent: *adj.* 回忆的，回忆往事的
3. Pablo Neruda: 巴勃罗·聂鲁达 (1904 – 1973)，当代智利诗人，1971 年诺贝尔文学奖获得者

年，无从走正当的司法程序。他说乔治·W·布什总统和托尼·布莱尔首相应该以战争罪受审。

根据品特的说法，绝大多数政治家对真相不感兴趣。

"他们只对权力感兴趣，"他宣称。他说，为了获取权力，维护权力，让人保持愚昧对他们来说很关键。

"我们被精心编织、无所不在的谎言包围着，"品特说。

品特用上流社会的口音（与其多部戏剧中着有效运用的伦敦俚语形成了对比），控诉英美两国在世界各地屠杀许多无辜平民。他说美国支持印度尼西亚、希腊、巴西、危地马拉、菲律宾和智利的独裁者。他说尽管成千上万无辜者在这些国家和其他地方被杀，即便这些悲剧还在上演，对他们来说也是"什么都没发生"。这个说法让人想起他的戏剧语言来。

品特以两首诗结束演说，第一首是巴勃罗·聂鲁达的诗，讲的是西

vilians during the Spanish Civil War. The second was his own poem, "Death". He had written this poem in response to the death of his father. In the context of his speech, it seemed both a protest against and an elegy[1] for the many deaths he referred to in describing the ruthlessness[2] of leaders in the United States and Great Britain.

The BBC, so loyal to Pinter early in his career, didn't broadcast his speech.

1. elegy: *n.* 悲歌，挽歌
2. ruthlessness: *adj.* 无情的，冷酷的

西牙内战中轰炸平民的行径。第二首是品特自己的诗《死亡》，他这首诗本来是写给自己死去的父亲的。但在演说中，这首诗显得像是抗议，抗议美英领导人的无情，也像是挽歌，纪念政客的无情所导致的无辜死亡。

而自早期以来一直忠实支持品特的BBC并未播放此次演说。

Chapter Twenty

MOONLIGHT

月光晚年

*T*he year after he won the Nobel Prize, Pinter went on stage again, this time as an actor. His last major public appearance was in Samuel Beckett's play, "Krapp's Last Tape". In October 2006, Pinter took the only role in this one-man play. This production was staged in celebration of the fiftieth anniversary of the Royal Court Theatre. All of the tickets for the limited number of seats and limited number of performances were sold out sixteen minutes after they were put on sale. People were eager to see the great playwright act in what was likely to be his last role. This choice of role for him was especially poignant. The title character, Krapp, is a lonely old man. He has no real life, only records of his memories. The play, by Pinter's good friend Samuel Beckett, had been written for another good friend, the actor Patrick Magee. Beckett's presence was in the words of the play, though he'd been dead seven years. Patrick Magee's presence was in the words of the play, too. He'd been the first actor to play the part of Krapp. Magee had been dead fourteen years at the time of this production. Everyone in the audience knew that Pinter was fighting a losing battle with illness.

The main action has the only character in the play listening to a recording of himself when he was thirty-nine. Pinter's own plays, many

获得诺贝尔奖的第二年，品特再次登台，这次是以演员的身份登台的。这也是他最后一次公开露面。他表演的是塞缪尔·贝克特的戏剧《克拉善最后的录音带》。2006年10月，品特演出了这部独角戏。这部戏是为了庆祝皇家宫廷剧院50周年纪念日制作的。限量发行的门票开始发售后，16分钟内便告售罄。人们都想目睹这位伟大的戏剧家演出人生的最后一个角色。品特演这个角色尤其让人悲伤。主人公克拉善是个孤独的老人，他没有真正的生活，只有关于他回忆的记录。品特的好友塞缪尔·贝克特是为另一位朋友、演员帕特里克·马吉写的这部剧本。贝克特那时已经逝世七年，但他的身影，仍出现在戏剧台词的字里行间。第一个扮演克拉善的演员帕特里克·马吉，也呈现在戏剧台词之间。这次演出时，马吉已逝世14年了。每位观众都知道品特正在与病魔作斗，且日渐不支。

戏中的主要动作是主人公在听他39岁时的录音。很多品特自己的戏

of them, anyway, were famous for their concern with memory. Neither Beckett nor Pinter emphasizes nostalgic[1] elements of memory. They emphasize its distortions and pathos[2].

The play's history and its content had special meaning for Pinter, as well as for those in the audience who knew him or his work. Henry Woolf, Pinter's friend from childhood days was there. Woolf had gotten Pinter his start as a playwright years ago. He had convinced his drama department to produce Pinter's first play, "The Room". Woolf himself was now seventy-six years old, the same age as Pinter.

"I felt a great sadness at the leaking of my own life into the eternal drainpipe," Woolf said, adding that he felt the same sadness for Pinter, as well.

Pinter's last performance was a moving one. He had gotten his start acting. This production did away with an element of slapstick comedy[3] that didn't fit the dignity of Pinter's situation and which would've required him to take a few steps. Pinter performed the entire monologue in his wheelchair. He stood only at the end to bow to the audience.

Reviewers praised the production. They spoke of his lean and sardonic interpretation of the role, of

1. nostalgic: *adj.* 思乡的,怀旧的
2. pathos: *n.* 悲伤，悲情
3. slapstick comedy: *n.* 打闹戏剧

剧都以记忆的主题而知名。但贝克特和品特都不强调记忆的怀旧成分，而突出记忆的歪曲与悲怆。

对于品特以及了解品特及其作品的观众来说，这部戏的历史和内容都对品特有着特殊意义。品特童年的好友亨利·伍尔夫也在观众之列。伍尔夫很多年前帮助品特成为戏剧家，他说服了自己就读的戏剧系演出品特的戏剧《房间》。伍尔夫和品特同龄，此时已76岁了。

"我感到很悲伤，我的人生在点点滴滴消失到排水管般的永恒之中，"伍尔夫说，他也为品特感到悲伤。

品特最后的演出很感人。他是做演员起家的。剧组删掉了一些打闹成分，因为它们不适合当时境况下品特。身体状况只允许他走几步。品特坐在轮椅上演出了整个独白，只在剧终站起来向观众鞠躬。

评论家盛赞此次演出。他们提到他对角色的演绎精到，且充满讽刺

his delighted attention to subtleties, like knocking a tape spool off the desk. People who came to see the play experienced an important moment in theater history.

During the next two years of his life, Pinter continued supporting political causes he believed in. He donated large sums of money to helping political prisoners who were subjected to torture. He signed petitions and lent his name to protests against war, including Israeli military retaliations[1] against Palestinians. He was true to his word, however, and never wrote another play.

Pinter faced death bravely, without the comfort of religion.

"I'm not afraid of dying," he told a reporter. "I think the heart stops and that's it, absolutely." He went on to say that he would, of course, regret leaving life.

Pinter had beaten his throat cancer, but cancer attacked him again. On Christmas Eve, December 24, 2008, he died of liver cancer. He was 78 years old. About fifty people attended his funeral a week later, on a cold, gray afternoon. The private funeral was held at Kensal Green cemetery, attended by family and friends. Many of Pinter's stepchildren and their children were there, but his own son was not.

1. retaliation: *n.* 报仇，复仇

性。他们还评论品特带着一种欣悦，关注戏剧的细微处，比如将一卷磁带从桌上甩到地下的一幕。这部戏是戏剧史上的重要时刻，能来经历的观众很幸运。

此后的两年，品特继续支持他所信仰的政治事业。他捐赠大笔钱给受到虐待的政治犯。他在请愿书上签名，表达对战争的抗议，包括以军对巴勒斯坦人的复仇行动。他说到做到，果然没有再写剧本。

品特没有宗教安慰，却也在勇敢地面对死亡。

"我不怕死，"他告诉记者。"我认为不过是心脏停止跳动而已。"他说当然，他会为离开人世而感到遗憾。

品特打败了喉癌，但是癌症又一次向他袭来。2008年12月24日，圣诞前夜，他死于肝癌，时年78岁。一周后，在一个寒冷灰暗的下午，50多人参加了他的葬礼。这次私人葬礼在肯赛·格林公墓举行，由亲友参加。品特妻子安东尼娅的子女和孙子孙女都参加了葬礼，但是品特自己的儿子却没来。

His son, Daniel Brand, was fifty years old at the time of his father's death. He hadn't visited Pinter for several years. Daniel left his father's last ritual[1] to his father's second family. During the last years of his life, Pinter missed his son, but couldn't find a way for them to reconcile[2]. Nonetheless, he spoke favorably and lovingly of his son, saying that he was brilliant, a gifted poet. He spoke, too, of the difficulty any child has in seeking to achieve his or her own success in the shadow of a famous parent.

Pinter's biographer, Michael Billington, thought some of Pinter's sadness about his son was echoed in the play, "Moonlight", his last full-length play. In this play, which premiered in London's Almeida Theatre in 1993, a dying man wants his sons to come visit him. They won't come. Only a daughter, Bridget, who is ghostlike, is present, though even she never actually comes into the father's room.

Her character brings to mind, St. Bridget, of Ireland, a patron saint of poets. In Irish mythology[3], Bridget was the goddess of fire and of poetry, as well as wisdom. She is associated with the bringing of light in wintertime. In the play, she is the character most closely associated with light. The character of Bridget is loyal to her parents, as the two sons are not, but she is

1. ritual : *n.* 仪式
2. reconcile : *v.* 使和解，使和谐
3. mythology : *n.* 神话

品特的儿子，丹尼尔·布兰德当时已经50岁了。他好几年都没去看品特。丹尼尔把父亲的最后仪式交给了父亲的第二个家庭。品特人生中的最后几年很想儿子，但是找不到和解的方式。尽管如此，提到儿子，品特总是充满赞赏和爱，说他是一个很出色、很有才华的诗人。他还说到，父母亲太出名，会给子女留下阴影，在这阴影下成就事业着实不易。

品特的传记作者迈克尔·比林顿认为，品特对儿子的悲伤在他最后一部独幕剧《月光》中有所反映。这部戏1993年在伦敦阿尔梅达剧院首演，剧中一个临死的老人想见儿子，但是儿子们都不愿来，只有一个幽灵般的女儿布里奇特来了，但连她也没进父亲的房间。

这个女儿的角色让人想起爱尔兰的圣布里奇特。圣布里奇特是诗人的守护神，在爱尔兰神话中，布里奇特是火、诗歌和智慧的女神，让人联想起冬天里的光明。在剧中，她是与光明紧密相关的人物。剧中，布里奇特这个人物忠于父母，而两个儿子却不。但布里奇特却如幽灵一

insubstantial, a ghostly presence. She's there, but not there.

In a way, this play seems emblematic[1] of the end of Pinter's life. It is a haunting play. Despite moments of comedy, it seems to represent the longing to connect emotionally with people we love as never completely fulfilled. Of course no single play can portray the complexity of the playwright. When Pinter was asked about why his plays were so violent and disturbing, he said he couldn't write a happy play. He said, on the other hand, that he had a happy life.

In the last half of his life, much of his happiness came from his wife Antonia's companionship. She was nearby when he wrote "Moonlight". In the play, the wife's name, "Bel", brings beauty and goodness to mind. Antonia, described as "golden" by one of her lovers, is a beautiful woman, who is described by Pinter himself in ways that suggest her good-spiritedness. Andy, the "A" of the play, is closest to the two "B's", Bel and Bridget. The two sons, Fred and Jake, are far away, physically and emotionally. In recalling Pinter's writing of this play, Antonia Fraser says that she asked him about Bridget's character. Because of her questions, he added a flashback of Bridget at a younger age. Antonia was pleased

1. emblematic: *adj.* 象征性的

般，其存在似有似无。

某种程度上说，这部戏是品特已近大限之日的象征。这是部让人难以忘怀的戏剧。戏里含有喜剧成分，但整部戏似乎是在表现我们想与所爱的人有所沟通，却无法实现这一愿望。当然，没有哪部戏能完全描绘出剧作家的复杂性。有人问品特为什么他的戏剧如此狂暴，如此令人不安，他说他写不出快乐的戏剧。可是他又说他一生生活幸福。

品特的后半生，快乐大都来自和他相伴的爱侣安东尼娅。创作《月光》时，她就在品特身边。在戏中，妻子的名字"贝尔"，让人想起美丽和善良。安东尼娅是个美女，一位情人形容她为"金色的"，品特的描述能显出她的快乐。戏剧中的主要人物安迪(A)和另外两个人物(B)贝尔(Bel)和布里奇特(Bridget)关系密切。两个儿子，弗雷德(Fred)和杰克(Jake)，则远隔千里，感情上也一样遥不可及。回忆品特如何写这部戏时，安东尼娅·弗雷泽说她就布里奇特这个人物问过品特。考虑到她提出的问题，品

that he took her questions into account in revising the play. She also took into account his questions about her work. She knew that if a passage wasn't clear to him, she'd better rewrite the passage — because he was an excellent reader. Both Pinter and Fraser often talked about their happiness with each other. After Pinter's death, Fraser said that she would write a memoir[1] about their life together. She said her husband was a great man. She felt privileged to know him.

Pinter's celebrity is worldwide. He is considered one of the greatest playwrights of the twentieth century. In addition to winning the Nobel Prize for Literature, the most prestigious award any writer can win, he has won numerous national and international awards for his plays. He was awarded eighteen honorary degrees from different universities. His influence is apparent on stage and in the movies. Important contemporary playwrights like David Hare[2] and David Mamet[3] give him credit as a major influence on their work. A journal, *The Pinter Review*, publishes theory, research, and interpretation in recognition of his artistic legacy.

1. memoir: *n.* 回忆录
2. David Hare: 大卫·黑尔 (1947–)英国剧作家，戏剧和电影导演
3. David Mamet: 大卫·马梅特(1947–)美国作家、散文家、剧作家、电影编剧和导演

特加入了布里奇特年轻时的一段倒叙。安东尼娅很高兴品特考虑了她的问题，并为此修改剧本。她也常考虑品特对她作品的建议。她知道，如果作品什么地方品特看不明白，她最好是重写——因为品特是个很出色的读者。品特和弗雷泽常常谈论他俩在一起的幸福。品特逝世后，弗雷泽说她想写一部两人一起生活的回忆录。她说丈夫是个伟人，她很荣幸结识品特。

品特享有国际声誉，他被认为是20世纪最伟大的剧作家之一。除了获得国际上最负盛名的诺贝尔文学奖之外，品特的剧本还获得了许多国内、国际奖项。他被18所大学授予名誉学位。他的影响涉及舞台和电影。当代重墨剧作家大卫·黑尔和大卫·马梅特承认自己的作品受品特影响巨大。《品特评论》期刊发表关于其作品的理论、研究、阐释文章，认可品特留下的艺术遗产。

The solitary little boy, who conjured imaginary friends near the lilac bush in the back yard of his home, grew up to people a unique world of theatre. Pinter's tragiccomic dramas have ugly and beautiful elements. As an author, he struggled to show the truth of human relationships, whether the truth was ugly or beautiful. He believed in his world, and liked his imaginary friends — his characters — to speak for themselves. Resisting analysis of his plays, he talked about his characters in terms of *what* they did, not why. In discussing a play with actors performing the roles, Pinter spoke of his characters as if they were real people. His affection for those "slightly desperate" make-believe friends testifies to a quality that enlarges his work. In combination with his artistic testimony[1] to human weakness and cruelty, he showed a tenderness toward his characters, an indulgence, like pale moonlight on a dark street.

1. testimony: *n.* 证言，证词

那个在自家后院丁香花丛梦想象出朋友的孤独小男孩，长大后，成就了一个独特的戏剧天地。品特那悲喜交加的戏剧饱含各种美与丑的元素。作为作家，他努力展示人际关系的真相，不论真相是美还是丑。他相信自己的世界，他喜欢那些假想的朋友——他的剧中人物——独立自主，有自己的看法。品特抵制对自己戏剧的分析，他只谈论人物做了什么，而不是为什么做。和演员谈论如何演出角色时，品特把人物当做真人来谈论。他喜欢他那些"略显绝望"的想象朋友，这种关爱证明了他有种特质，正是这特质让他的作品如此伟大。他用艺术手段见证了人类的弱点和残忍，除此之外，他还对剧中人物流露出了柔情和关爱，这柔情，这关爱，正如黑暗街道上那抹淡淡的月光。

Bibliography
参考书目

Baker, William. *Harold Pinter*. London: Continuum, 2008.

Billington, Michael. *The Life and Work of Harold Pinter*. London: Faber and Faber, 1996.

Burkman, Katherine. H. *The Dramatic World of Harold Pinter: Its Roots in Ritual*. Columbus, Ohio: Ohio State University Press, 1971.

Burkman, Katherine H. and John L. Kundert–Gibbs (Eds.). *Pinter at Sixty*. Bloomington, Indiana: Indiana University Press, 1993.

Dukore, Bernard F. *Harold Pinter.* (Modern Dramatists Series), New York: Grove Press, Inc., 1982.

Gale, Stephen. H. *Sharp Cut: Harold Pinter's Screenplays and the Artistic Process*. Lexington, KY: The University Press of Kentucky, 2003.

Pinter, Harold. *The Birthday Party and Other Plays*. London: Methuen, 1960.

Pinter, Harold. *The Caretaker*. London: Methuen, 1960.

Pinter, Harold. *The Dwarfs*. New York: Grove Weidenfeld, 1990.

Pinter, Harold. *The Homecoming*. London: Methuen, 1965.

Pinter, Harold. *Moonlight*. New York: Grove Press, 1993.

Pinter, Harold. *Mountain Language*. London: Faber and Faber, 1988.

Prentice, Penelope. *The Pinter Ethic:The Erotic Aesthetic*. Studies in Modern Drama, Vol. 3. New York: Garland, 1994.

Ziegler, Philip. *London at War*. New York: Alfred A. Knopf, 1995.